CW01266892

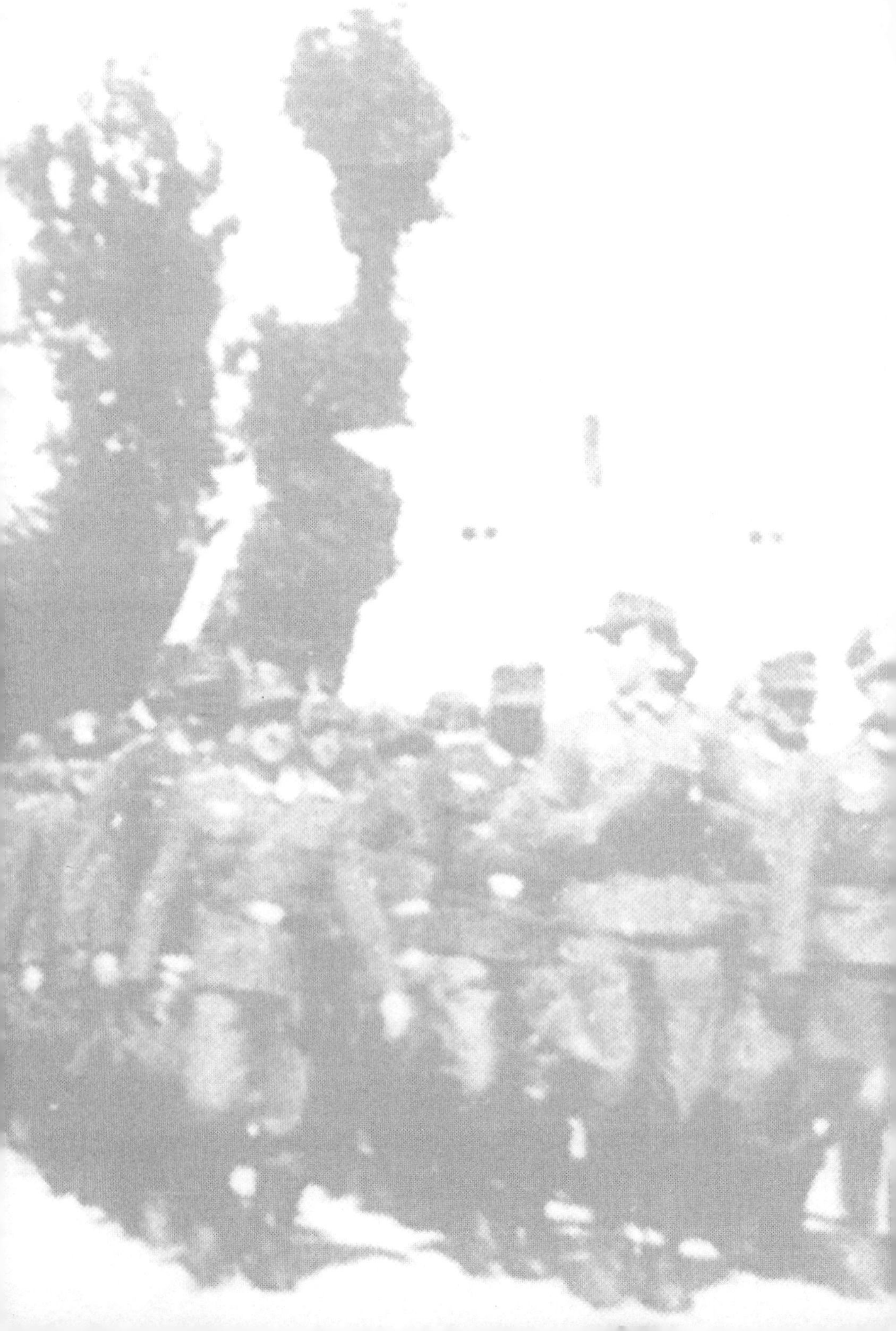

ASPECTS OF WAR

A social history of the German Occupation of the
British Channel Islands
1940 to 1945

Written and compiled by

JUNE MONEY

First published in three books between 1993 and 1995.

This revised edition in one volume
published in 2011 by Channel Island Publishing,
Unit 3B, Barette Commercial Centre, La Route du Mont Mado,
St. John, Jersey JE3 4DS

CHANNEL ISLAND PUBLISHING

Copyright © 2011 June Money
All rights reserved

No part of this publication may be reproduced, stored in a retrieval system or transmitted in any form or by any means electronic, mechanical, photocopying, recording or otherwise without the prior permission of the author.

ISBN 978-1-905095-36-0

www.channelislandpublishing.com

Aspects of War was first published in a series of three books, specifically designed to provide a social history of daily life experienced by the people of the Channel Islands under the German occupation during the period 1940 to 1945 in WWII. The idea was developed in consultation with the Education Development Centre, Guernsey, under the guidance of the working group of G.A.T.O.H (Guernsey Association of Teachers of History).

Acknowledgements:
The author wishes to express her grateful thanks to the following for helpful information and advice given in the original three-part compilation of this book, and for the loan of material.

John Blampied, Jersey

John Bouchere, Jersey

Peter Dobson, Guernsey

W.R.B. Giffard, Sark

Michael Ginns, Jersey

Guille-Alles Library, Guernsey

Richard Heaume, Guernsey

Mrs. Dorothy Hurrell-Langlois, Guernsey

Mrs. Dawn Madell, Guernsey

Mrs. Miriam Mahy, Guernsey

Mrs. D. R. Mees, Guernsey

Mrs. Pearl Regan, Guernsey

J. T. Renouf, Jersey

Dr. John Renouf, Jersey

Mrs. Janet Rolfe, Guernsey

Peter Sarl, Guernsey

Doug Tanguy, Jersey

Ken Tough, Guernsey

Mrs. Janet van Zanten, Guernsey

I also acknowledge those people, sadly no longer with us, for their valuable contribution to my research undertaken for the original three-part series: Bill Green, Len Dorey, Peter Girard, Bill Mahy, Barbara Newman, Gladys Skillett, Freda and Percy Ozanne, and Edward Peadon.

Credits:

For permission to reproduce copyright material, thanks are due to:

Channel Islands Occupation Society, Guernsey (CIOS Guernsey)
Channel Islands Occupation Society, Jersey (CIOS Jersey)
German Occupation Museum, Guernsey
Guernsey Island Archive Services
Guernsey Evening Press
Jersey Evening Post
Jersey Library and Société Jersiaise, Jersey
Priaulx Library, Guernsey, for the Carel Toms Photographic Collection and the B. C. De Guerin Scrapbook

Grateful thanks are also extended to other numerous people who gave their time so willingly to talk about life and conditions under German Occupation.

Front cover photographs

March past, Jersey 1944
C.I.O.S. Jersey Collection

German troops on their way to British p.o.w. camps after Liberation.
Carel Toms' Collection

Contents:

PART I - EVACUATION AND ENTERTAINMENT
Introduction
The Evacuation
A Matter of Luck - A short story depicting life under German Occupation
Radios
Cinemas
Theatre
Music
Dancing
Sport
Home Entertainment

PART II - FOOD, CLOTHING AND DAILY LIFE
Food
Cooking
Fishing
The Black Market
Rationing
Bartering
Clothing
Make Do and Mend
Footwear
Tobacco
Health
Education
Red Cross Parcels

PART III - DAILY LIFE AND LIBERATION
Transport
Fuel
Communications
    Newspapers
    Resistance News Sheets
    Radios
    Red Cross Letters
Deportations
Internment Camps
Liberation

PART I
ENTERTAINMENT
AND PASTIMES

Introduction
The Evacuation

A Matter of Luck -
A short story depicting life under German Occupation

Radios
Cinemas
Theatre
Music
Dancing
Sport
Home Entertainment

INTRODUCTION

When war was declared between Britain and Germany in 1939, it had no immediate effect on the daily life of Channel Islanders. They were confident that Britain's military strength would keep them safe as had been the case in the 1914-1918 war.

The situation changed with the invasion of Holland, Belgium and Luxembourg. The fall of Paris in the middle of June 1940 and the advance of German armies towards the coast were of even greater concern.

The British government was indecisive about the defence of the islands. Of little strategic importance, they would be difficult and costly to defend. Should they be demilitarised, there was every hope that the war would pass them by.

Urgent talks took place between the islands' representatives and the Home Office in London about the possibility of demilitarisation. The islands' authorities were informed of the Government's decision on 19 June. Regular troops, including those who had escaped to the islands from France, left for England together with the Guernsey and Jersey Militias on 20 June. Newspapers carried notices that the UK Government was to provide ships for the voluntary evacuation of women and children, men of military age (20 to 33-year olds) and, if room allowed, other men.

Unfortunately the British government did not immediately inform the German government that the islands had been demilitarised. They were afraid that the withdrawal of British troops might be regarded by Hitler as an opportunity to invade them. Also they assumed that Hitler would be aware of the situation through his own intelligence network. The delay was fatal. Forty-four people died on 28 June 1940 when armed German reconnaissance planes bombed and machine-gunned the towns and harbours of St. Peter Port in Guernsey and St. Helier in Jersey. Many more were injured. The surrender of Guernsey took place on 30 June 1940 followed by Jersey on 1 July, Alderney on the 2nd and Sark on the 3rd.

Imagine life today without television, DVDs or radio. During the five years' German occupation of the Islands the only form of entertainment available to the population was that produced by the islanders themselves. It played an extremely important part in boosting flagging morale. D-Day, which took place on 6 June 1944 with the Allied landings in Normandy, was responsible for all forms of public entertainment being closed down. Some cinemas were later allowed to re-open and to operate until the Liberation, depending on electricity supplies.

Charles Gardner, who was a well-known musician and entertainer in Guernsey, wrote: 'With the British and American invasion of the north-west of France in June 1944, all amusements and theatres were closed down, leaving us with absolutely nothing to do but . . . read!!' (Source 21)

THE EVACUATION

In Guernsey plans prepared by the Education Department for an evacuation of school children were immediately put into action. Children whose parents had consented to their departure were collected from schools the next day and taken to the harbour by bus. (Source 1)

Women with children under school age, expectant mothers (Source 2) and men of military age (Source 3) who had registered their names were given permits to depart. Many other people, alarmed by the stream of French refugees arriving in the islands, had already left fearful for their safety. In all 19,000 people out of a population of 43,000 in Guernsey were evacuated, of whom 5,000 were children.

With the departure of the Lieutenant-Governor, Major-General Minshall Ford, on 21 June, the Bailiff, Victor Carey, who was 70 years old, was sworn in as the civil Lieutenant-Governor in Guernsey. On the same day the States of Deliberation (the Island's government) set up the new Controlling Committee. This committee was given power to make swift decisions in the event of occupation. Attorney-General Major Ambrose Sherwill, a much younger man, was elected President.

It was a difficult period with insufficiently strong leadership. The confusion spread to Alderney, the second largest island in the Bailiwick, approximately 5.6 by 2.4 kilometres (three and a half miles long by one and a half miles wide) in size. The population was 1,400 before the emergency. A break-down in communications between Ambrose Sherwill and Judge Frederick French, Chief Administrator of Alderney, hampered the evacuation considerably.

A ship eventually arrived amid fears and rumours on 20 June, with instructions to evacuate school children and teachers only. When it returned to Guernsey with few people on board, Major Sherwill, unaware of these instructions, assumed that the rest of the population had decided to stay, and no other evacuation ship was sent. This mistaken idea was given further support when an urgent request for yeast to make bread was later received.

Food was running out, but the crew of the regular supply ship refused to sail as Alderney was only eight miles from the coast of France. The *Vestal* arrived on 21 June to pick up the Trinity lighthouse keeper, and the captain offered to take on board 150 civilians. Judge French, afraid of a stampede, declined but asked the captain to relay a message to the Admiralty. In it he requested the evacuation of all remaining 1,100 civilians if there was a definite danger of invasion. Six ships arrived the next day and only 20 people stayed behind. They were later forced to leave the island and taken to Guernsey, but one family, George and Daphne Pope, four of their children, Mrs. Pope's mother, Violet Gordon, and a farmer were given permission to return. Together with an Alderney fisherman who had managed to evade being apprehended in the first place, they remained the only civilian residents for the remainder of the occupation where, in addition to a lack of food, other hardships included no medical support, no formal education for the children and of course no shops.

Alderney became the blackest spot in the history of the occupation when the Germans built four hard labour camps, Borkum, Helgoland, Norderney and Sylt, to house mainly political prisoners and prisoners of war, which included Russians, Ukranians, French, Spanish, Jews and many other nationals. These prisoners were used to build fortifications on the island. They received the harshest of treatment and were reduced to near starvation. Many died.

The tiny island of Sark, which lies just over 11 kilometres east of Guernsey, had been ruled by Dame Sybil Hathaway since 1926. The feudal ruler took a strong view on the evacuation: 'We may be hungry. But at least there will always be fish and rabbits.' She did not foresee that fishing was to be severely restricted and that there would be under German rule no guns to shoot the rabbits. Apart from the English residents and a few holiday makers, the 471 Sarkees decided to stay at home.

In Jersey, Alexander Coutanche was sworn in as the civil Lieutenant-Governor on the departure of Lieutenant-Governor General Harrison. As in Guernsey, the States Assembly (the Island's government) set up a Superior Council and elected Alexander Coutanche as President. He handled the evacuation and threat of occupation with clear directives. Out of a population of 50,000 people, 23,000 registered for evacuation. Between 10,000 and 11,000 eventually departed.

Considerably fewer people left Jersey than the smaller island of Guernsey, and they included only a few children.

The first steamers, small and hopelessly inadequate for the transportation of so many men, women and children, eventually arrived in Weymouth. There they had to wait 24 hours or more to disembark as the port was congested with ships and refugees from Bordeaux. To make matters worse their food ran out. Once ashore and examined by medical and immigration officers, people with private means and accommodation were allowed to depart.

The majority of school children were sent to Cheshire, Lancashire, Yorkshire and Scotland. Following long and tiring train journeys, they were taken to centres where they stayed until they could be billeted with families. Some schools were fortunate to remain together. Many parents, following their children on later boats, lost contact with them for several months.

The Channel Islands Refugees Committee was set up in London at the beginning of July. Within a few months £25,000 had been raised to help those in need of assistance. The Channel Islands' Monthly Review was published by the Stockport and District Channel Islands Society, maintaining a precious link between the refugees.

Telegrams and messages of the safe arrival of school children and other evacuees were sent back to the islands. Many of the messages were printed in the newspapers for the comfort of those left behind.

With the evacuees safely away, those remaining in the islands attempted to carry on as best they could. Between 5,000 and 6,000 cats and dogs had been destroyed in Jersey and 2,000 in Guernsey. But there were still abandoned farm animals to take care of and empty properties to be made secure. There was also a perishable food surplus to be dealt with, brought about by the evacuation of so many people. Food rationing which had been introduced to cover the crisis was suspended on these items.

Although the demilitarisation of the islands effectively took place on 19 June, news of it was suppressed by the Home Office. A reason given later was the need to keep the escape route for British soldiers from St. Malo open for as long as possible. All British troops, however, had been withdrawn from France by 17 June. Another reason was the government's anxiety that the Germans should not regard the demilitarisation as an opportunity to walk in. An assumption was also made, incorrectly, that German intelligence would have become aware of the military evacuation.

Had the British government notified the Germans earlier, it is possible that the deaths of 44 people might have been avoided. As it was, on 28 June 1940 the German Luftwaffe attacked the harbour and town of St. Peter Port in Guernsey, killing 33 civilians and wounding many others. (Source 4) In Jersey the main area of attack was La Rocque and the harbour of St. Helier, where 11 civilians were killed and again many wounded. It was only then that the Home Office ordered the BBC to announce that the islands had been demilitarised. News of the bombing was released the following day. But it was not until 30 June that the Foreign Office asked the US Embassy to pass a message on to the German government in Berlin, that the islands were undefended.

The Germans occupied Guernsey that same day. An ultimatum for a peaceful surrender was dropped on Jersey on 1 July. The deserted island of Alderney was taken over by a small detachment of German troops on 2 July and a sergeant and 10 soldiers were billeted on Sark on 3 July. (Source 5) In the space of four days nearly 900 years of ties with England had been severed.

A MATTER OF LUCK
A short story depicting life under German Occupation

Betty placed the earphones of the crystal set over her ears and carefully prodded the tiny crystal with the small piece of wire. 'Do hurry up, Pearl,' she said at last. 'I've found the station and the latest tune is on now. We could use it in the new show.' (Source 6 and 9)

'Just a minute,' Pearl said. 'We've got to make sure there are no Germans about.'

Betty frowned, as she watched her elder sister cross the sitting room to the door. Much to the family's dismay, their hotel had been commandeered by the Germans soon after the occupation began. It was awful having enemy soldiers living under the very same roof as themselves, but they knew that to protest would mean their being forced out of their home. Where would they go? There was certainly not room enough for four extra people in their grandparents' small cottage. So then, an abandoned house perhaps? But that would most likely have already been looted, the occupants having fled the island to the mainland before the invasion. In the end the family had decided to remain at the hotel where at least they would be able to keep an eye on their property.

Now, since German officers had been billeted on them, the family could never be sure at what time their unwelcome guests might return.

'If they find the crystal set we'll be in terrible trouble,' Betty whispered. 'Mum and Dad as well.' Her eyes widened with fear. 'Since all our radios were confiscated we could end up in prison, or even get deported to Germany for defying the order.'

'Well, they haven't found it so far,' Pearl said and stuck out her chin. 'Anyway I find it all rather exciting.'

'Well I don't.' Betty shuddered. 'As for the shows, my legs turn to jelly when I see Germans in the audience. What can we say if they ask us how we know the latest tunes from England?'

Pearl shrugged. 'We'll say we heard them on the wireless sets the Germans use here in their rooms.'

Betty continued to look troubled. 'They'll never believe that. And what about the gun? The one that I found last night between the seats at the theatre at the end of the show?'

'Why should you worry? You handed it in at the German Headquarters.' Pearl opened the door and peered into the empty hall. 'Perhaps you should have kept it.'

'Don't joke about it,' Betty said crossly, grabbing a cushion and throwing it at her.

The Germans were always so suspicious about anything unusual. Her parents had been taking part in a variety show which she and her sister had watched from back stage. She had been helping to clear the auditorium at the end of the performance, and the moment she had found the pistol she knew it would bring trouble. A German officer sitting in the audience had dropped it between two of the seats. To think that she had brandished it in fun at the rest of the cast, not realising it was loaded. She had handed it in all right, but not until after she might have shot someone with it.

'All clear,' Pearl said, shutting the door and turning the key in the lock. She threw the cushion back at her sister and, picking up a pencil and paper, sat down beside her. 'Good old BBC. I'll jot down the music. Thank goodness I have learnt to read music. You write down the words.'

Sharing the earphones, the two girls nodded and swayed to the lively rhythm, until a loud rapping on the door had them leaping to their feet. There was no time to hide the crystal set under the floorboards and Pearl hid it in the only place she could think of.

'Okay,' she hissed, 'you can open the door.'

Betty recognised the tall grim faced German officer waiting outside. 'Fraulein Elizabeth Le Sauvage?' he asked in a very stern voice.

She nodded, too frightened to speak and watched him stride into the room. He sat down heavily on the couch, crushing her mother's best satin cushion.

'It has been reported that you . . .' The two girls trembled whilst he studied a piece of paper in his hand. '. . . you handed in a pistol.' Betty swallowed hard and nodded her head. 'So then you will accompany me to our headquarters where you will answer some questions.'

'I found it, that's all, Herr Leutnant,' she whispered, remembering to use the form of addressing a German officer with the rank of lieutenant. Her face was white with fear. 'I don't know anything about it.'

'Possession of a firearm is a serious matter,' the officer insisted. 'You will come with me now.'

'But my sister is only sixteen,' Pearl protested. 'Please wait while I get my father.'

'It is not necessary,' the officer said briskly and got to his feet.

Nearly in tears, Betty followed him to the door. Pearl tried not to look scared. 'There's nothing to worry about Betty,' she said. 'You've done nothing wrong. As soon as I find Dad he'll go straight down to headquarters.'

She hovered at the window and watched her sister climb into a waiting car. The moment it was gone she ran to the couch and lifted the cushion. The crystal set was completely flattened. The weight of the officer had almost destroyed it and she knew it would take hours for her father to repair it. It had been a matter of luck that the officer had not found it.

She hid the set beneath the floorboards and ran from the room to look for her father. Now they must pray that their luck would continue.

RADIOS

Up to September 1940 islanders were permitted by the German authorities to listen to the BBC (British Broadcasting Corporation) broadcasts, (Source 7) but sets were then confiscated as a reprisal against islanders for help given to British agents, Second Lieutenants Hubert Nicolle and James Symes, when they landed secretly on Guernsey to make a survey of the island. The sets were returned to the population in December 1940, but taken away again in June 1942 for military reasons until the end of the war. Some islanders, determined to outwit the German military order, kept their wireless sets hidden, whilst many others acquired or made crystal sets to listen in secret. (Source 8) The BBC had broadcast instructions on how these simple receivers should be made.

The crystal receiver was known as the Cat's Whisker. Hardly any two sets were alike. Usually they consisted of a coiled wire, with one end wound into a terminal and the other attached to a set of headphones. Another short piece of wire – the whisker – was left free to tune into the crystal. (Source 9)

It was possible to make a crystal by mixing the shavings from an old silver threepenny piece with sulphur, placing this in a small container, such as a spent bullet case and heating it in a fire until it exploded. A less dangerous method was to heat lead and sulphur in a saucepan until it formed into small balls. Alternatively a small piece of coal with a gold vein running through it could be used, if such a piece could be found.

A special high powered radio station was set up by the BBC at Start Point in Devon on the south coast of England. (Source 6) From this station it was possible to pick up reception on the crystal sets. The coil on the set was wired to the wavelength frequency. To tune into the station it was necessary to prod the crystal with the whisker until the right spot was found.

Later when there was no electricity with which the Germans could operate their own radios in the islands, many of them made crystal sets themselves – but the only station they could get was Start Point!

One illegal radio was hidden in the console of the cinema organ in the Regal Cinema in Guernsey. (Sources 10, 15 and 16) It was in full view of German troops twice daily when the organ was played by the organist, Kennedy Bott, but fortunately for the cinema manager it was never discovered.

The manager of Wests Cinema in Jersey was not so fortunate. He was arrested for possessing a radio and deported to a camp in Germany. For islanders to be caught in possession of either a radio or a crystal set it was an offence against the German authorities and punishable by a fine or, worse still, imprisonment. In one particularly severe case in Jersey in 1941 a father and son were arrested and deported to Germany where, sadly, they died.

In the island of Sark, part of the Bailiwick of Guernsey, however, the German Commandant chose to ignore a notice pinned to a tree listing

Entertainment and Pastimes

the names of people who had not turned in their radio sets, declaring it to be the work of a traitor. (Source 11)

There were a number of cases throughout the islands in which some treacherous islanders tried to avenge themselves on fellow islanders by informing on them. The German authorities made it quite clear that they disliked being used in this manner.

Throughout the occupation no direct broadcasts were made to the islands by the BBC, although the islands were mentioned in programmes wherever possible. Because of this many islanders felt their plight had been abandoned by the British government. In fact the BBC broadcasts had been restricted because of fear of reprisals on the population by the German authorities.

CINEMAS

Cinemas operated in the islands throughout most of the occupation, until they were closed at intervals by order of the German Commandant after D-Day in June 1944. (Source 12)

An evening at the cinema could sometimes be a risky affair. In the early months of occupation, civilians had applauded the British forces and booed Hitler when they appeared on the screen. Subsequently, under a threat of severe penalty, audiences were not allowed to applaud or comment during a cinema performance. Notices were posted in the foyers of the islands' cinemas to this effect. (Source 13)

When the Germans, however, realised that the notice banned all applause they hastily issued a further notice, giving permission for audiences to applaud the heroes of feature films and comedians! And it was most certainly compulsory to applaud Hitler!

German forces and civilian audiences were segregated by order of the German commandant. Notices were put up in foyers of cinemas to this effect, although frequently programmes were set aside on certain days for the sole entertainment of the occupying forces. Balconies were usually reserved for officers and their guests but, where there were none, in some cases dividing rails were installed. (Sources 14 and 15)

Eventually there was an exchange of English films between Guernsey and Jersey. Islanders, however, soon lost interest in the small stockpile which had been left behind at the beginning of the occupation. German films, filled with propaganda and carrying English sub-titles were imported for the troops and also shown to decreasing civilian audiences. It was then that the theatre became really popular.

The Forum Cinema in Jersey and the Regal Cinema in Guernsey, later re-named the Odeon, were taken over by the German authorities for their sole use. (Source 16 – note the wall built in front of The Regal Cinema to protect the foyer from bomb blasts and gunfire). On occasion, permission for civilian use was granted for special presentations.

Variety turns and artists were occasionally brought over from Europe by the Germans. On one particular occasion the Regal Cinema was used by a German variety star to entertain the troops with his marksmanship. After the liberation of the islands five bullet holes were found in the screen, left there one night when his aim was so poor he missed the target of a lighted candle five times. It was fortunate that no one was in the dressing room at the side of the stage at the time as one of the bullets penetrated that too! (Source 17)

THEATRE

Professional and amateur artists performed together in musicals, concerts, variety shows and plays in all the islands. Standards in stage productions and performances rose to a high level (see Source 18) and the talent of local playwrights and composers grew in response to the demand by islanders for more and more entertainment. The opening of each new show was a great event. During the course of the occupation, hundreds of shows were produced in the islands' theatres and parish and church halls (Source 20).

A great deal of skill and inventiveness was required in making costumes from unwanted clothing and any pieces of oddments that could be found. In one production in Jersey two suits of armour were required and these were made by a plumber from flattened tomato puree tins. Rubber inner tubes were used for the skirt and sprayed with silver paint. The fittings for the armour had to be carried out with metal snips – hand shears for metal cutting. (Source 19)

Stage make-up was available in the islands at the beginning of the occupation but later additional supplies came from France.

All scripts and programmes were censored. The contents of newspapers, books, scripts, films, etc., had to be examined by the German press censor, who was also the entertainments officer, before public release. On occasion words, phrases, and sometimes whole sections of a script could be severely cut to remove any material offensive to the German authorities. (Source 18)

Entertainment and Pastimes

In this connection no mention of the British Royal Family was allowed except in prayers. In one musical production a theatrical company in Jersey submitted the music for a march entitled 'For King and Country'. It was immediately censored. The musical director of the show, Jack Le Mouton, re-scored it on lined manuscript paper and re-titled it 'The Jack Le Mouton March'. It was passed by the censor without any further comment.

Lack of transport and curfew (the time determined by the German authorities for all islanders to be indoors) made it difficult for many islanders living outside the towns to visit the theatres. Whenever possible the established theatre companies in the islands took the shows to the outlying parish and church halls. Many of the churches became focal points for amateur dramatics and sport.

It was normal for each theatrical company to apply for an extension to the curfew so that audiences did not have to rush home after a performance. The commandant might grant an extension for the last night of the performance, or even a couple of nights, but if permission was not granted he never gave a reason. On one occasion, a matinee performance was given at half past ten in the morning so that the evening performance could commence at half past six.

There was always a risk, too, that the German authorities might take over a theatre or a hall at the last minute for their own requirements. (Source 18) When this happened there was a frantic last minute search for an alternative venue, but the show went on if at all possible.

Unlike in Guernsey and Jersey, censorship on the tiny island of Sark was not quite so strict. At the commencement of the occupation the German authorities had considered that one commandant and a token force of approximately ten soldiers was sufficient strength to be stationed there. The population numbered approximately five hundred people. The troops were only greatly increased up to a maximum of five hundred soldiers after several secret landings made by British commandos.

As long as the Sark Amateur Dramatic Society adopted a sensible attitude to the content of the scripts and programmes, they were free to put on stage productions much as they pleased. As there was no cinema on the island the Sarkese relied on these productions greatly for their entertainment.

MUSIC

The Germans enjoyed listening to military bands and put on open air and indoor concerts whenever the opportunity arose. The rousing music could often be heard in the streets, town squares or from bandstands. In Guernsey the Candie Auditorium, where the Candie Museum and Cafe now stand, and in Jersey the Royal Square and The Parade were particularly popular venue. (Source 22 and 23)

Sadly the German hostility and prejudice against Jewish people (their anti-semitism policy) banned the performance of any music written by Jewish composers, among them being compositions by Mendelssohn.

Some islanders in defiance of the German authorities played Beethoven's Fifth Symphony. The opening bars of the music represent the Morse Code (dot dot dot dash) – V for Victory! All victory signs were a source of great annoyance to the Germans and culprits were severely punished. These opening bars also preceded the BBC Forces' News on the radio.

DANCING

It was only a short time after the commencement of the occupation before dance classes in tap, modern and ballet began to be re-established. Pupils took part in many of the concerts and theatrical productions and several dance mistresses put on their own shows. As ballet shoes became scarce pupils had to practise in bare feet, keeping the few available ballet shoes for actual performances. A prominent dance teacher in Guernsey, greatly involved in the theatre during the occupation, commented on the number of healthy young feet which came out of this practice.

Ballroom dancing was not very popular at the commencement of the occupation and for a time dances were banned by the German authorities. They were afraid that the troops, whilst mixing with the civilians, might accidentally give away military information. By 1942, however, private dances were being arranged (Source 24).

In the summer of 1943 dances and all other forms of public entertainment were banned in Jersey on medical grounds to prevent the spread of disease. Diphtheria was one of the main problems and parents were urged to have children inoculated. One hotel advertised a ballroom dance as a dancing class, but the Germans were not fooled by this trick and it was cancelled.

SPORT

Athletic meetings, tennis tournaments, football matches, table tennis and netball (Source 26) were all important activities in the islands whilst equipment was available. As tennis shoes and plimsolls wore out and there were no new ones available to replace them, any form of footwear that could be found was used. Even bedroom slippers and rope-soled sandals were better than nothing. But later when these also could not be replaced some sports were played in bare feet.

Tennis became almost impossible to play when balls became scarce and court nets were removed by the Germans for military purposes – possibly for camouflage.

Boxing tournaments were so popular that tickets were an immediate sell-out as soon as they were announced. Although in Guernsey the Germans sometimes gave permission for a tournament to take place at the Regal Cinema (Source 25) most of them were staged at the Lyric Theatre in New Street. For perhaps the first time in the history of the theatre the boards had to be scrubbed after each tournament by staff to remove any blood that may have been spilled before the next stage production could go on!

Football was particularly popular and attracted large numbers of spectators and supporters. The islands' Occupation cup match was played each year and the final in 1944 was watched by between four and five thousand people. At times matches were arranged between the civilians and occupying forces, but the majority of games were played between the civilian teams.

The welfare of the islanders had always been the concern of both islands' medical officers of health. As early as after only one year of occupation it was strongly recommended that competitive sport should no longer continue. The general shortage of food and rationing had caused an insufficient balance in diet, and energy had to be conserved (Source 26).

Despite this recommendation and the islanders' determined efforts to continue with sport as long as possible, they were finally forced to give up due to lack of food. They did not have the strength to carry on and all forms of sport were finally totally discouraged.

HOME ENTERTAINMENT

Reading was popular but the German authorities censored many of the books and had them removed from library shelves. They insisted that islanders should learn their language. To encourage them, magazines were placed in libraries and simple German lessons were printed in the islands' newspapers. (Source 27)

Card games, such as whist and euchre drives (in which four players, two in partnership, take as many 'tricks' as possible, with the winning hand on each round gaining points) were popular entertainment in the home. Musical evenings were also enjoyed and the most popular instruments were the piano, the violin, the accordion and the mouth organ. House parties would sometimes continue late into the night, despite the curfew, and then guests would have to remain with their hosts until morning. Even so there are many tales about islanders who took the risk of breaking the curfew and yet managed to get home safe and sound.

A couple on one such occasion were returning home from a party at the late hour of two o'clock in the morning. Suddenly to their horror they heard the sound of heavy footsteps approaching and hastily jumped over a hedge. After the unsuspecting sentry had passed them by, they rose to their feet and with a shock found themselves face to face with two equally frightened German soldiers. With a sign to remain silent the soldiers waved the couple on their way and then took off in the opposite direction back to their barracks.

Entertainment and Pastimes

Source 1: Schoolboy waiting to be evacuated. Note the label on his coat and the cardboard box containing a gas mask.
German Occupation Museum

Source 2: Women and children in Guernsey awaiting evacuation to England
Photograph: Carol Toms Collections

Below
People in Jersey waiting to board a ship to the UK
Photograph: Societé Jerseiaise

Aspects of War

Source 3: Men of military age preparing to leave Guernsey to volunteer for the British Forces. *Photograph: Carel Toms Collection*

Source 4: The remains of the sheds on the White Rock, St. Peter Port, Guernsey after the German air raid on 28.6.1940. *Photograph: Carel Toms Collection*

Entertainment and Pastimes

Source 5: German soldiers marching along The Avenue in Sark.
Photograph: *Carel Toms Collection*

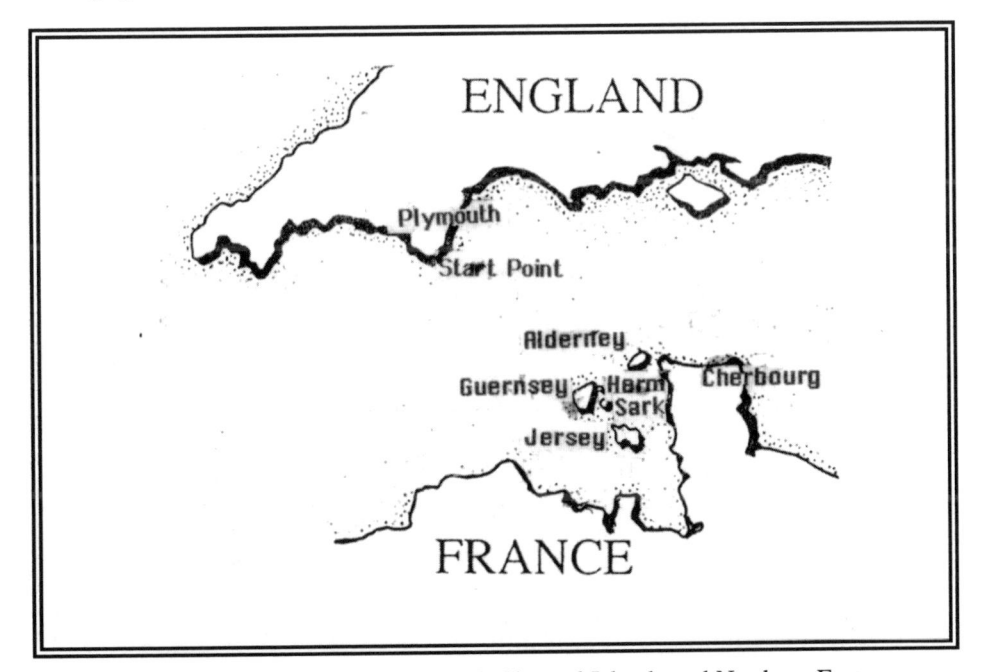

Source 6: Map showing Southern England, Channel Islands and Northern France. Note Start Point in Devon on the South coast of England, where the BBC set up a special high powered radio station.

RIGHT

Source 7: BBC radio programmes published in Guernsey Evening Press dated 17.8.1940.

ABOVE

Souce 8: Listening to an illegal crystal set hidden in a tomato chip basket.
Photograph: *German Occupation Museum*

B.B.C. RADIO PROGRAMMES

We publish to-day the Home and Forces Programmes radiated by the B.B.C., through the kind permission of the German Commandant.

HOME SERVICE
(German Time)

2.0—News; 2.15—Backs to the Land; 2.35—Tudor Sextet; 3.0—Royal Horse Guards; 3.45—Hymns we love; 4.0—Music while you work; 4.30—Fleet Street Choirs; 5.0—Concert Party from the West; 5.30—Six Counties at War; 6.0—News and talk in Welsh; 6.20—Children's Hour; 7.0—News; 7.30—News in Norwegian; 7.45—Women and War; 8.0—Saturday's Spot Light; 8.30 Symphony Concert; 9.15—Music Hall; 10.0—News; 10.15—To-night's Talk; 10.35—Home Coming; 11.15—Evening Prayers; 11.30—Gaelic Service; 11.35—Dance Music; 12.55—Bedtime Reading; 1.0 a.m.—Midnight News.

FORCES PROGRAMME
(German Time)

2.45 p.m.—" Accent on Rhythm "; 3.0—Time Signal. Band of the Royal Horse Guards; 3.30—Popular songs on gramophone records; 4.0—Music while you work; 4.30—Canadian Concert Party; 5.30—Records of old favourite songs; 6.0—Orchestral Concert; 6.40—" The Old Country." Scottish songs and dances; 7.0—News in Dutch and French; 7.30—Organ recital; 7.45—Fred Hartley and his Sextet; 8.30—John Rorke. Recital; 8.55—Herman Darewski and his Band; 9.15—News in French; 10.15—" Let 'em all come." The Colossal Stores entertain their Staff.

(Change to 342 metres.)

11.0—Sandy Macpherson at the organ; 11.20—The story of Stanley Lupino told by records; 11.45—Dance Music.

Source 9: Two examples of the Crystal Set –The Cat's Whisker
German Occupation Museum

Source 10: Kennedy Bott at the Compton Organ, Regal Cinema, Guernsey in which an illegal radio set was hidden in the console. *Photograph: Author's Collection*

Source 11: Traitor's Tree – The Avenue in Sark – to which was pinned a list of names of people who had not handed in their wireless sets. *Photograph: The Carel Tom's Collection*

Entertainment and Pastimes

Bekanntmachung	NOTICE
(1) Um elektrischen Strom zu sparen, werden ab sofort sämtliche Theater und Lichtspielhäuser geschlossen, sowie alle Tanz- und sonstigen öffentlichen Veranstaltungen eingestellt.	(1) With immediate effect all theatres and cinemas will close down in order to save electrical energy. All dance and other public entertainments are cancelled.
(2) Die Sperrstunde wird auf 22.00 Uhr vorverlegt. Die Wirtschaften haben um 21½ Uhr zu schliessen.	(2) Curfew hour is advanced to 10.00 p.m. Restaurants and public houses must close at 9.30 p.m.

Der Platzkommandant,

HEIDER,
Major.

Platzkommandantur I St. Helier.
7. Juni 1944.

Source 12: Notice of closure of all theatres and cinemas in the Channel Islands following D-Day

---

Nebenstelle Guernsey
der
Feldkommandantur 515

O.U., den 7.11.40.

An den Präsidenten des Controlling Committee
of the States of Guernsey.

Betr.: Demonstrationen bei Vorführung
von Filmen.

Bei den Kinobesitzern ist zu veranlassen, dass diese das Publikum durch Anschlag in den Vorräumen auf die Unzulässigkeit von Beifalls- oder Missfallensäusserungen bei der Vorführung von Filmen aufmerksam machen.
Zuwiderhandlungen werden mit sofortiger Schliessung auf 8 Tage geahndet, die Anstifter streng bestraft.
Mit der Durchführung und Überwachung dieser Anordnung ist die Inselpolizei zu beauftragen.

I.V.

Kriegsverwaltungsassessor.

Re: Demonstrations during the showing of films.
Instructions should be given to Picture House Proprietors to notify the Public by means of notices posted in the halls that no demonstration of approval or the reverse will be tolerated. Contraventions will result in 8 days closing and the instigators will be severely punished.
The Island police shall see to the compliance with this regulation.

Source 13: Letter to the president of the Controlling Committee States of Guernsey concerning demonstrations by audiences during the showing of films. *Guernsey Island Archives Service*

Aspects of War

NOTICE

For German films with English sub-titles the left-hand section of the stalls are reserved for Civilians only; the right-hand section and the Balcony for German troops only.

Source 14: Notice segregating the German Forces and civilian audience in one of the cinemas and the Gaumont Cinema in Guernsey showing 'Victory in the West' a Nazi propaganda film

Entertainment and Pastimes

The Operator was Imprisoned—the Manager Hid a Radio Set in the Organ—and the Show went on

B. C. de GUERIN
"Kine." Guernsey Correspondent

OF the six kinemas in the Channel Islands, the Germans only actually took over control of one—the Regal, in Guernsey—during the whole occupation. True, their national flair for meddling in other people's affairs was displayed by interference with all forms of entertainment. But, though they compelled the other kinemas to show German films, sometimes at weekly intervals and sometimes interspersed with British programmes, the Regal was the only house completely under their direct supervision.

During the raid upon St. Peter Port which preceded the actual landing of the Germans in 1940, and in which many civilian lives were lost, the Regal was showing, appropriately, the Laurel and Hardy film, "The Flying Deuces."

Closed by order of the local authorities, as were all entertainments after the raid, the Regal was ordered by the Germans to reopen within 48 hours of their occupation of the island.

Foresight Helped

Fortunately, through the foresight of Lou Morris, the managing director, there was a stock of stand-by features sufficient to keep going, without repetition, for five weeks. Then the German invasion spread to the picture houses, and they assumed control of the Regal. Retaining the manager, Eric Snelling, a peace time member of the KINE. Company of Showmen, and his civilian staff, they began by giving two nights a week to German films. Troops were admitted free to these shows, but civilians paid. By the end of 1941 the programme was entirely German and no civilians were admitted.

This arrangement lasted until the Liberation, with various alarms and excursions in the interval. D-Day was one of these, after which event the Germans removed to the Lyric, which was more conveniently placed in a side street and therefore not such an easy target for the Allies' Air Forces as the more imposing but isolated Regal.

Electricity Cut Off

In November of last year electricity was cut off from all theatres to conserve the dwindling resources of power. There was thus a period without film shows, but on March 1, 1945, the Germans resumed their performances at the Regal, allocating a block of 200 seats for the use of civilians.

The Last Days

During the last few days of the Occupation the Regal was utilised for a purpose which is surely unique. Officers of the German garrison were summoned there on several occasions to be addressed by the island commander, Admiral Hoeffmeyer, a fire-eating Nazi, who exhorted them to resist the British landing and to fight to the last man. Apparently none appeared anxious for the honour, and despite the eloquence of the Admiral, the officers decided to go quietly.

The passing of "Jock" Kerr, manager of the Gaumont in Guernsey, which occurred on June 3, 1944, was a great shock to all who knew him. Due directly to malnutrition, his health gradually gave way, and after a short period in hospital, he died at the age of 61.

After D-Day

Shortly after D-Day the Gaumont closed down for the remainder of the Occupation. The Germans had always insisted on a varying proportion of their films being shown there, and half the house was reserved for their troops.

The North Cinema was unfortunate in that its proprietor, Deputy Chas. Cross, was among those residents who were shipped away to internment camps in Germany for no other crime than having been born British. After his departure the Germans compelled Eric Snelling to supervise and manage this house in addition to the Regal and the Lyric.

Throughout the Occupation, amateur theatrical companies were popular with the islanders, and some very creditable performances were put on. These, together with boxing shows, local variety turns, and concert parties, kept the ball rolling, and Eric Snelling succeeded in extracting the necessary permission to use his theatres for such shows when occasion arose. He thus did much to keep fellow-islanders from a complete mental "black-out" during the great ordeal.

For the last three years of the Occupation the Germans prohibited the possession of wireless sets among the civilian population. Needless to say, many still retained them. Amongst these was Snelling who, with the organist at the Regal, W. Kennedy Bott, had an all-mains set concealed in the console of his theatre's Compton organ. Thus, twice daily when the organ came up to be played, the forbidden set was displayed in full view of about 700 Germans—and not one of them saw it!

Well Behaved

On the whole, the invaders were a well-behaved audience. Seating accommodation was "zoned" by their Press Censor, who was also Entertainments Officer, and soldiers, marines, officers and bearers of special passes were all segregated like sheep in their pens. Here some of the more destructive used their bayonets to slit the plush arm-pads and extract the rubber cushions, which they used for boot-repairing. Nearly a thousand arm-rests suffered in this way during the five years. Carpets also vanished under the iron heel of the invader.

Roy Machon, operator at the Regal, was sentenced to nine months' imprisonment in a German prison in France for making "V"-sign brooches out of shilling pieces, and after completing his sentence was confined in an internment camp in Germany.

Everyone else on the staff, from manager to attendants, has been accused on different occasions of "sabotage."

Yet, despite these drawbacks, and others which arose from the general conditions prevailing on the island, such as lack of fuel and heat for the last two winters, the show went on. The spirit of the traditional showman somehow survived.

Source 15: Cutting from Kinematograph Weekly dated 21.6.1945. *(B.C. de Guerin Scrapbook)*

Source 16: The Regal Cinema, Guernsey. Note the bomb blast protection covering the entrance – a wooden frame covered with corregated iron and packed with sand. *Photograph: Guernsey Evening Press* and The Forum Cinema, Jersey *Photograph: Michael Ginns*

German Shot Holes in Screen

FIVE bullet holes were found in the 26 x 20 foot Westone screen of the Regal, Guernsey, when this was dismantled and replaced by a new one. The old screen had done service, with one application of spray to its surface, since the cinema was built in 1937, including five years of German occupation.

During this time a German marksman punctured the screen, though this was not a mark of disapproval. It was the bad marksmanship of a variety star imported for the amusement of the troops.

His "stunt" was shooting out a lighted candle from the back of the hall. On one particular night the marksman missed his target five times. The bullets, besides perforating the screen, also penetrated a dressing-room in the rear of the stage. No one was in it at the time.

Source 17: Cutting from Kinematograph Weekly 21.6.1945. *B.C. de Guerin Scrapbook*

Entertainment under the Nazis

by BASIL C. de GUERIN

A Channel Islander sends this account of the splendid part played by the theatre in the Channel Islands during the grim years of the German Occupation.

THE German Occupation of the Channel Islands had the effect of stimulating that love of the theatre which was always an outstanding feature of the social life of the islands.

After the initial period of adjustment of existence to the rule of the Nazi, the public began to tire of the cinema, with its compulsory injections of German propaganda and, as no alternative was possible to procure from an outside source, sought the remedy in its own ranks.

The search was definitely successful, both as to quantity and quality.

On Guernsey alone no less than five distinct companies of players; two casts for musical comedies; a stock variety company; and numerous concert parties were all well patronised on each of the frequent occasions on which they appeared.

It was estimated that when all these groups were at the height of their activities, during 1943, that a total of some 500 persons were engaged in the entertainment of their 20,000 fellow-islanders.

Audiences and local newspapers alike were critical, and that the former were by no means confined to relations and friends of the players is shown by the figures of one entertainment committee who, in a 19 week season, put on 75 performances by 8 concert parties before a total attendance of 75,000 persons. The record single attendance at these was 7,100, when £145 was taken for charity.

Among the 'legitimate' companies a very high average of ability was established and maintained, and one or two 'discoveries' were made that might yet bear fruit if transplanted to wider fields. Virtuosity was encouraged and ambition led to the presentation of some real 'test' plays, which were however, on the whole, successfully negotiated.

Of these *Night Must Fall*, *Ghost Train*, *A Murder has been Arranged* and *The Wind and the Rain*, must be mentioned as the high-water mark of Guernsey's "Regal Players," who also put on eleven other plays, varying in degree both in substance and in execution.

Light comedy was the aim of the remaining companies, and they achieved their object with commendable regularity.

Both Jersey and Guernsey were fortunate in the possession of their own local playwrights and composers, and each island was thus able to stage some very ambitious and colourful revues in which the choreography was a home product well up to professional standard. Casts of over 50 were accommodated in these, the only limitations placed upon the ambitious novice being those of stage space.

Although each of the two islands possessed at least one theatre suitable for any style of entertainment, it was never possible to rely upon the use of any particular venue too far ahead. The Germans were liable to step in at any moment and commandeer it for the use of their own travelling troupes of players. If, on doing so, they found anything not to their satisfaction, such as lack of heating in the dressing-rooms at a time when the islanders were totally without fuel, then the Manager was accused of 'sabotage,' a charge which covered a multitude of sins.

German censorship was also strict. The script of all proposed plays, and entertainments generally, had to be passed by the Nazi Press Censor who was also Entertainments Officer and was not always blessed with an appreciation of the British sense of humour. In such circumstances it was not a pleasant job for a producer to have to go through the entire book of say, *Charley's Aunt* or *Tons of Money* before a hard-faced audience who was scared to death of having his leg pulled and possessed the power of jailing the unfortunate reader if his suspicions were aroused.

The islanders have every reason to thank those who gave of their time and their gradually dwindling energy to the entertainment of their fellows. Without such distractions life would have been even more grim than it was during those five long weary years, for the last three of which all wireless sets were forbidden to the civilian population.

It is proposed that certain of these local companies shall continue now that the Liberation has lifted the mental black-out. There are many players who will be welcomed back to the boards again and, good as they were during Nazi domination, they should go to far greater heights now that the atmosphere is once again cleared.

Source 18: Cutting from Theatre World October 1945

B.C. de Guerin Scrapbook

Entertainment and Pastimes

Source 19: Drawing of a suit of armour on which a stage costume might have been based.

Source 20: Poster of the Charity Show for the Help-the-Children Fund, presented at the Regal Cinema ('by kind permission of the German Commandant') on 5 July 1943
German Occupation Museum

Aspects of War

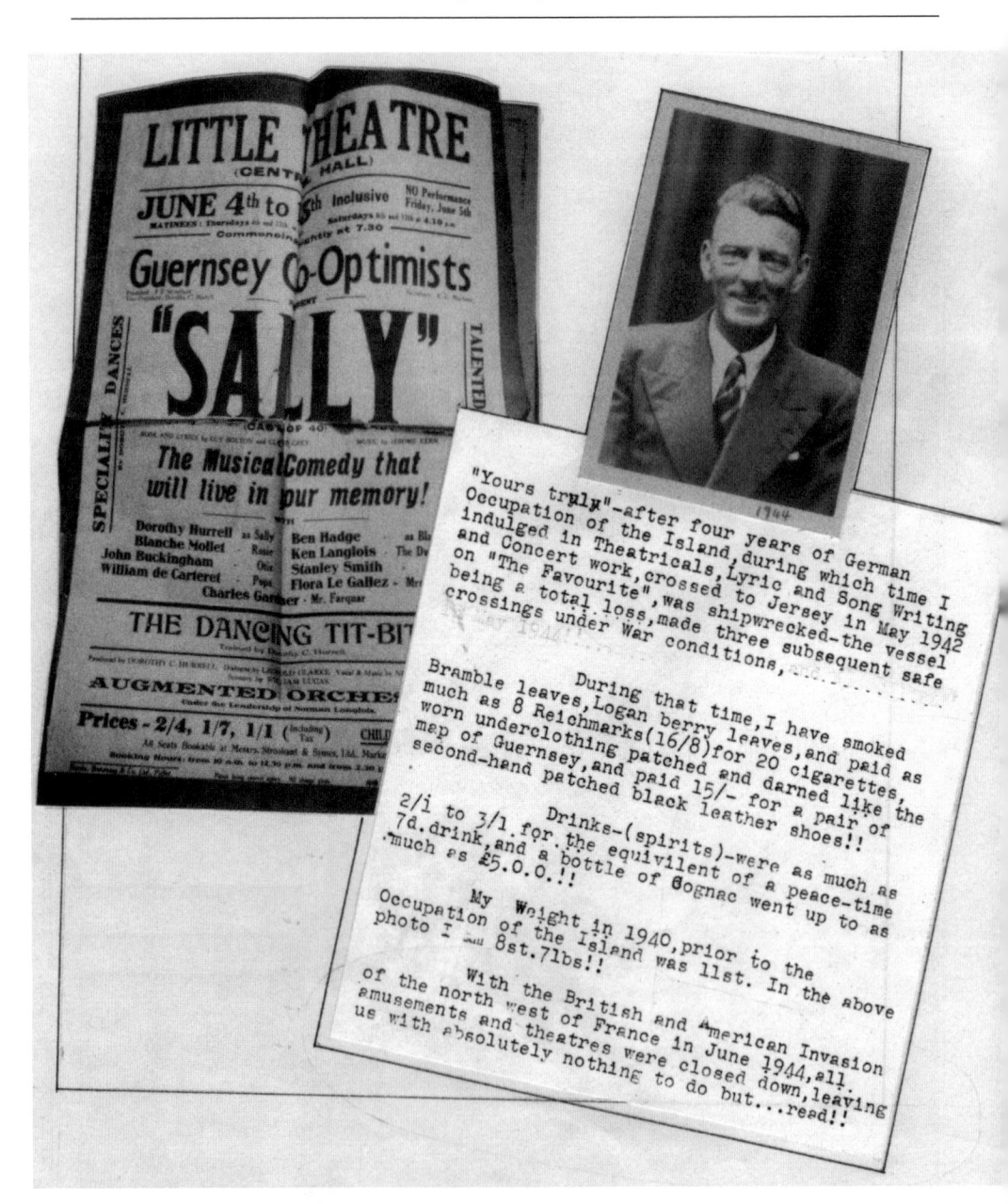

Source 21: Poster and diary note from the scrapbook of Charles Gardner, a Guernsey entertainer. *Courtesy: Mrs. Dawn Madell, Guernsey*

Entertainment and Pastimes

Source 22: German soldiers and civilians listening to a German Military Band concert at the Candie Auditorium, Guernsey *Photograph: Guernsey Evening Press* and a German Military Band in the Parade, Jersey Photograph: *Société Jersiase*

Source 23: German Military Band playing at the Weighbridge in St. Peter Port, Guernsey. Note part of the name of London and Manchester on the building in the background. Published in a German magazine this would give readers the impression that Hitler's troops had landed in Britain. *Photograph: Mrs. Janet van Zanten, Guernsey*

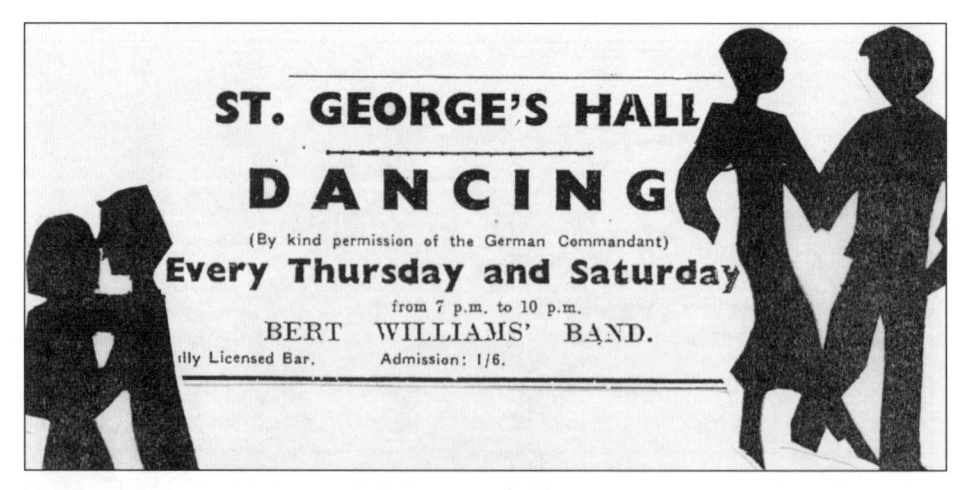

Source 24: Notice appearing in Guernsey Evening Press 17.8.1940

Entertainment and Pastimes

REGAL
Guernsey's Finest Cinema — Gas, Manager: E.K. Bradley

The Guernsey Amateur Boxing Committee presents a

BOXING TOURNAMENT

MONDAY, OCTOBER 25th, 1943, at 6.45 p.m. sharp.

AMATEUR BOXING COMMITTEE:
President — Mr. Vin Golling
[officials list partially illegible]

KENNEDY BOTT AT THE ORGAN.

2/4

NETBALL

It is good news to see that netball is to be revived among girls of 14 years of age and over. As a means of mildly strenuous physical exercise netball is an excellent game and is ideal for growing girls.

Many teams have participated in the past, and we hope the efforts at a revival will be successful. With the reconstruction and adjustment of the educational system of the island in accordance with the number of children now upon it, there should be scope for many netball teams and even those who have left school and are still willing to play will be found a place if they will get in touch with any of the following ladies:—

Miss Anderson, St. Martin's School, or 2, Escallonia, Mount Durand.
Miss C. Bichard, Hautgards, Vale.
Mrs. Wellington, Clifton School of Commerce, Grange.

SPORT

IDEAS FOR SOCCER SEASON

LABOUR DEPARTMENT BACK FOOTBALL

(By "Achilles")

About a fortnight ago I wrote in the sporting columns that I considered that sport should be organised in Guernsey on the same lines as in Jersey where the Labour Department has taken over the sporting programme. My article was read by the Labour Organisation officials here and the idea has had a certain amount of appeal. It has been taken up by Deputy Wilfred Corbet, who is assisting Deputy R. H. Johns at the Labour Bureau. Deputy Corbet takes a great interest in sport and the youth of the Island and so it is very likely that things will begin to move before long and by the time the winter reaches us plans for the soccer season should have been formulated.

I had an opport[...]

Source 25: Poster advertising a Boxing Tournament to be held at the Regal Cinema, Guernsey, 25 October 1943 *German Occupation Museum*

Source 26: A few weeks after the commencement of the Occupation, these sport items appeared in the Guernsey Evening Press. Eventually all form of sport was discouraged Guernsey Evening Press 17.8.1940

Aspects of War

TO-DAY'S LESSON IN GERMAN

No. 29 OF OUR SERIES.

More useful phrases in English, with the German translation, approximate pronunciation in English spelling, and German pronunciation in English.

ENGLISH.	GERMAN.	PRONUNCIATION.
1 Has there been an accident?	Ist ein Unglück geschehen?	Ist ine Oonglück geshayn?
2 A car has run into a tree.	Ein Auto ist gegen einen Baum gefahren.	Ine owtoh ist gaygen inen Bown gefahren
3 Has a doctor been called?	Hat man einen Arzt geholt?	Hat man inen Artst geholdt?
4 Show me the way to the Hospital.	Zeigen Sie mir den Weg nach dem Lazarett.	Tsygen Zee meer den Vayg nach dem Lazarett.
5 Straight on, keep to the right.	Gerade aus, halten Sie rich rechts.	Gerahder ews, halten Zee sish reshts.
6 Is anybody hurt?	Ist jemand verletzt?	Ist yaymand ferletst?

AUSSPRACHE DES ENGLISCHEN.—1 Has zhär bien en achsident? 2 E kar has rönn intu e trie. 3 Has' e docter bien kold? 4 Schoh mi zhe uäi tu zhe Hospitl. 5 Streht onn, kiep to zhe reit. 6 Is enibodi hört?

Source 27: German lesson appearing in Guernsey Evening Press 17.8.1940

PART II
FOOD, CLOTHING AND DAILY LIFE

**Food
Cooking
Fishing
The Black Market
Rationing
Bartering
Clothing
Make Do and Mend
Footwear
Tobacco
Health
Education
Red Cross Parcels**

Immediately prior to the German invasion Jersey had formed the Superior Council under the presidency of the Bailiff, Alexander Coutanche. In Guernsey the Controlling Committee had been set up by the States of Deliberation under the presidency of H.M. Procureur, Ambrose Sherwill. These two islands' governments administered the two bailiwicks throughout the entire occupation. They made every effort to keep the people fed and in as reasonable health as possible under the eagle eye of the German military authority.

There was no immediate shortage of food after the invasion as rationing of existing stocks had already been put into effect. The islands were not self-supporting, having largely relied on imports from the UK. As an example annual food imports in Guernsey had amounted to 16,636 tons. Therefore, unless arrangements were made to import essential items from France, serious shortages could be expected throughout the islands before the end of winter.

Jersey had normally grown substantial outdoor crops of potatoes and tomatoes and was less reliant than Guernsey on glasshouse production owing to a good deal of her arable land facing south. Guernsey on the other hand, being a much smaller island and with a northern aspect, had been largely dependent on producing crops of tomatoes and flowers under glass. Now Jersey was to concentrate on wheat, oats and barley, vastly reducing her potato crops, whilst Guernsey was to convert most of her glasshouses from tomatoes and flowers to vegetable growing.

The 471 inhabitants of Sark grew almost sufficient vegetables to feed themselves for the greater part of the war. Even so they did not escape hunger and hardship, having to wage a continual battle against rats and rabbits eating valuable crops and to supplement the rations of German troops stationed on the island. Poultry and rabbits were kept in pens and cages, and rabbits in the wild were caught and eaten.

Alderney, which was to become the blackest spot in the history of the occupation, had been almost totally evacuated on 23 June 1940, leaving behind only 20 out of a population of just over 1,100. One hundred and fifty head of cattle were shipped to Guernsey and distributed to farmers. Later, after the arrival of the Germans on 30 June, a small party of workers was sent from Guernsey to Alderney to clear up the mess left by the fleeing evacuees and to salvage anything of use. (Source 3)

During the period 1941 to 1942 it was decided to make use of the arable land in Alderney to grow food for Guernsey. A group of States workers was sent to gather the harvests and a herd of cows was imported from

France. Another party of Guernseymen and Sarkees worked on the breakwater. From 1943, when Alderney became a fortress island and a camp for forced labourers and prisoners, the Germans took over the growing of food for themselves and the working parties returned to their home islands.

Milk rationing was introduced throughout the islands in October 1940. People in Guernsey over the age of fourteen were allowed half a pint of skimmed milk daily. In Jersey the daily allowance for everyone over the age of 16 was half a pint of full cream milk. Overall there was a larger ration of full cream milk for children, nursing mothers and invalids. The decision not to slaughter the dairy herds for meat was taken because of the importance of the production of milk, butter and cheese.

Surplus potatoes and tomatoes were exported from Jersey and Guernsey to France in return for the necessary supplies which had previously been obtained from the UK. Soon after the occupation commenced, Mr. Raymond Falla from Guernsey (later awarded an O.B.E.) and Mr. John Jouault from Jersey were authorised to set up a permanent purchasing commission in France. The headquarters were established in Granville under the supervision of a German official.

This hard working commission was a life-line to the islands. The agents worked seven days a week, travelling great distances in an effort to obtain whatever food and other essential commodities they could find. The commission continued to operate in Granville until the allied invasion of France in June 1944, which eventually made it necessary for them to move to St. Malo. (Source 4) There they had to stay until the liberation of the islands in 1945.

Raymond Falla used to entertain people for many years after the war with an amusing story about an incident which occurred during his stay in France. It happened on one particular occasion whilst he was eating a meal in a restaurant reserved for German troops. It appeared he had a remarkable likeness to Hitler. Suddenly to his horror the diners began getting to their feet and giving him the Nazi salute. Having no right to be there in the first place, he left rather hurriedly before the situation really got out of hand.

SUBSTITUTE FOODS

Islanders experimented with substitutes for food and beverages that were in short supply or no longer available.

Coffee:	Acorns, parsnips, sugar beet, barley, wheat, beans and lupin seeds – roasted and ground. (Source 5)
Tea:	Bramble leaves, green pea pods, camellia leaves, lime blossoms, carrots and parsley – shredded and baked. (Source 6)
Salt:	Seawater – evaporated. (Source 7)
Gelatine:	Carrageen moss, an edible seaweed – dried and bleached. (Source 8)
Flour:	Potato flour mixed with ordinary flour for making bread. Also used for puddings and thickening stews and gravies. (Source 9)
Sugar Beet Syrup:	Sugar is contained in the root of the beet. (Source 11)

To obtain the syrup the roots were cut into cubes, covered with water and cooked in a large pan or a washing copper for five or six hours until they were tender. They were then put through a press. The juice was collected in a tray beneath it. (Sources 10 and 12) The juice was then boiled down until it formed into a light treacle, care being taken that it did not burn and spoil the flavour. It could also be thickened with carrageen moss rather than by boiling down the syrup, but the quality was then lost.

COOKING

Increased rationing of fuel caused many difficulties with cooking. The committees of the islands' essential commodities urged people to take uncooked food to bakehouses. There for a few pence it was cooked overnight after the day's bread had been baked.

Communal kitchens were established in Jersey very early in the occupation but were not set up in Guernsey until much later. A communal kitchen in St. Helier had served over 400,000 meals to the people by the end of 1943. That same year the States food distribution department had served 1,359,449 pints of soup to the public and 648,435 pints to schools.

Furze ovens, many of which had not been used for years, were brought back into use, both in domestic households and bakehouses. (Source 13) Furze, or gorse, was forked into the oven and burnt until the bricks inside appeared white hot. Ashes were then raked out and food placed inside to cook for two to three hours.

Cooking was also done on open hearths. An improvised oven and pots and kettles were placed on a simple metal stand. (Sources 14 and 15)

Hay box cookery was a great saver on gas and electricity (Source 16 and 18) particularly when the services were cut to a few hours a day. Food requiring long slow cooking was brought to the boil on a conventional stove or a fire and cooked for a short time. It was then transferred to a hay box. A galvanised iron dustbin packed with straw was also used in hay box cooking.

Sawdust stoves were simple to make and widely used. When there was no form of fuel for heating or cooking at all, people were forced to eat food raw. (Source 19)

FISHING

The Germans were forever afraid that civilians would try to escape from the islands, taking with them military information. For this reason, and with the danger of mines in the water, fishermen were not permitted to take their boats beyond one to one and a half miles from shore without a German escort. With an escort, the distance varied at times up to a three-mile limit. Boats were allowed to leave the harbours one hour after sunrise and had to return one hour before sunset, but they were not allowed out in fog or rain. In addition to all these rules twenty per cent of each catch had to be put aside for the German Forces.

In the early stages of the occupation fishermen in Sark were allowed to put to sea between 10am and 3pm. Obviously, when tides were unsuitable they did not work. It took a few months for the German officers who gave the order to realise that 'time and tide wait for no man'. The Sarkees must have enjoyed a good laugh when their unwelcome visitors were forced to reconsider the matter.

Fishing in the islands was totally banned in September 1940 as a result of an escape by eight Guernseymen in a twenty-foot fishing boat. (Source 22) The ban was lifted a couple of weeks later, after the order came for all boats to be moved to the main harbours. (Source 20) Despite

Food, Clothing and Daily Life

these punishments attempted and successful escapes continued, including that of Jerseyman, Dennis Vibert who, on his second attempt in September 1941, reached England in an eight-foot dinghy. He rowed for four miles before switching on one of the two outboard motors. During a storm when one engine failed and the other was lost, he was forced to row for three days and nights without food. He was picked up on the third night just off Portland by the Royal Navy. (Source 21)

In July 1942, as a further security measure, fishermen were ordered to paint bands of blue, white and red inside and outside their boats, so that they could be easily identified from above. (Source 23)

Fishing at sea was by permit only. These were issued to married fisherman who had no relatives or children in England. Fear that families left behind would be punished made their escape less likely. Single men were considered a higher risk and excluded.

Three more escapes in August 1943 resulted in another ban on fishing until security arrangements were tightened even further. Bonds (deposits which could be forfeited) of up to £100 (RM1,000 – Reichsmarks) a boat and £50 (RM500) a fisherman were imposed and fishing was allowed only in groups under German escort. With so many restrictions it was not surprising that fish accounted for a very small part of the diet.

Rod fishing was allowed without a permit on authorised beaches between 6am and 8pm. (Source 24) As food became even harder to find people searched the seashore for winkles, sand eels, limpets, razor-shells and ormers when available. (Source 25)

Limpets are tough and had to be minced, stewed or casseroled. Large quantities were also used to feed dogs, cats and poultry. The Germans found ormers tough and inedible, having no idea that they should first be carefully beaten to soften the 'foot' (the hard muscled centre) before they were cooked.

Razor-shells, known locally as razor fish, require patience to catch as they withdraw themselves rapidly into their deep holes in the sand, using their muscular foot. One way to catch them was to push a piece of hooked wire down the holes in the sand made by them so that it passed between the two shell valves. The razor fish could then be carefully drawn back up. Apart from digging for them with a spade, another method was to sprinkle salt down the holes. This was much slower, but the razor fish would eventually come to the surface.

THE BLACK MARKET

By 1942 food and general items were in short supply and many things had run out. Some unscrupulous islanders seized the opportunity to make money out of the situation. Prices on the black market were out of all proportion. The islands' courts did everything they could to stamp out the illegal trading and gave harsh sentences to any offenders they managed to catch. In Jersey the military tribunal of the *Feldkommandantur* sentenced four Guernseymen to prison for periods between five and twelve months, and imposed heavy fines. (Source 26)

Despite efforts to discourage the black market, it became firmly established, supported by the people who could afford to pay. Those without money and the few who would have nothing to do with it went without.

The black market was not confined to the civilian population. Many of the Germans, including some of the *Feldgendarmerie* (the German Military Police) were involved and this underlines the inherent injustice of law under occupation. Although it must be said that a German official, Kurt Goettmann, who had been the press censor in Guernsey, was brought to trial in Germany by his superiors, stripped of his rank and sentenced to three years' imprisonment for black marketeering and various other crimes.

The captains and crews of ships and barges sailing backwards and forwards to the French ports also dealt in the black market. Even many of the Organisation Todt workers (forced labourers brought over to work on the fortifications), who had been fortunate enough to make a brief visit to their homes, smuggled easily carried foods, such as butter, eggs, saccharin and other small items on their return.

Black market prices rose steadily throughout the occupation and became excessive. By 1944/1945 butter was costing as much as £2.50 a pound. Even more astonishing was the price of tea which reached prices between £20 and £30 a pound. Eggs in 1944 reached approximately 35p each. When compared to a farmhand's weekly wage in 1941 of less than £2 and a skilled engineer's weekly wage of less than £3, it can be seen just how high the prices demanded were.

Farm animals, such as cows and pigs, had to be registered with the Farm Produce Board (Source 27) which kept a strict control on all livestock and produce. The natural or unexpected death of any farm animal had to be reported and investigated immediately. As the majority of farmers were involved in the illegal slaughter of animals at some time or another, mostly in order to feed themselves and their families as well as supply the illegal meat

Food, Clothing and Daily Life

trade, they used various tricks to hide their crimes. Sometimes they would keep the carcass of a dead animal which had already been officially inspected and recorded as deceased to use again for inspection in place of another cow or pig intended to be illegally slaughtered.

Farmers managed to get round this regulation in one way or another. One man in Guernsey instructed a farmhand to load a pig onto a horse-drawn cart and not return to the farm until after a count had been taken by an official from the farm produce board. Another devised a plan to steal his own cow by making a false report. Having arranged for a trusted friend to hide the animal for him, he reported the 'theft' to the authorities. Unfortunately it was before his friend had had a chance to complete the task!

Another tale that came to light in Jersey at the end of the occupation was that of a pig, hidden under a blanket and carried by stretcher into the operating theatre of the hospital. Once safely inside a butcher quickly cut it into joints.

RATIONING

For the purpose of rationing the Channel Islands were included in the Manche district of France. The purchasing commission, which had been set up by Guernsey and Jersey in August 1940 to buy food and other necessary commodities in that area, dealt with the French government official in charge of that district.

All food (with the exception of vegetables and fruit), clothing and footwear were allocated by ration cards. (Source 31) In general people living in the country parishes were better off for vegetables than townspeople who did not have enough land to grow any quantity.

Shops and markets, which had thrived before the occupation, were now empty most of the time. As soon as food appeared in them there were long queues of people waiting to be served. Often long before the end of a queue had been reached there would be nothing left to sell. (Source 28)

As stocks dwindled, so the Germans commandeered more food until eventually at the end of 1944 they were so low that there was barely enough to maintain a reasonable state of health. (Source 29) By order of the German authorities civilians of German origin residing in the islands before the arrival of occupying forces were entitled to receive extra rations. This was discontinued when the Red Cross parcels arrived as, much to the islanders' disgust, these people were also entitled to receive them, although the German troops were not.

The Sark food committee was set up in July 1940 to control the use of agricultural land and to deal with the island's requirements. A herd of 150 head of cattle supplied the milk, which was rationed at half a pint of full cream for children and one pint for adults. Other supplies were shipped from Guernsey, normally about three times a week.

Stocks of soap were exhausted in Jersey by February 1941 and in Guernsey by June of the same year. (Source 30) Substitute soap was imported from France but was of poor quality. It had no lather and produced an unpleasant smelling slime. Each bar of toilet and household soap was rationed at four ounces a month with additional rations for babies and hospitals. To make the soap go further it was boiled with ivy leaves. Selected mud, wood or fine sand were also sometimes used as soap substitutes. Those who could afford the black market prices bought it when it was available.

Clothing and footwear coupons (Source 31) were used throughout the occupation. Even after liberation rationing continued for another few years until supplies were restored to a normal level. Working clothes were allocated by parish in the larger islands. (Source 32)

BARTERING

By the end of the first year of occupation food, clothing and other essential commodities were scarce. People bartered amongst themselves, through the shops and through advertisements placed in their local newspapers. Anything they could spare was exchanged for something they needed more urgently. (Sources 33 and 34) Amongst items to be found listed in the Guernsey Exchange and Jersey Exchange and Mart columns were such things as a rabbit for a pair of good working shoes, a gents' bicycle for a ladies' bicycle and a nightgown for flour and sugar. Although restrictions were placed on the barter of rationed goods in Jersey in 1941, they were not imposed in Guernsey until the beginning of 1942.

Many shopkeepers with no goods left to sell allowed their premises to be used by the general public as exchange locations. No money was involved. The value of an item was shown by the value of an article wanted in exchange. The shopkeeper received a percentage of the value of the article at the time the exchange took place.

CLOTHING

Within a few months of the occupation it became obvious, after inventories of clothing and footwear had been taken, that rationing of these items had to be introduced immediately. Shopping hours were limited to four and a half hours a day on three days week.

The Summerland Factory re-opened in Jersey for the manufacture of clothes and knitwear. Guernsey's smaller workshops turned out many clothes and undertook all kinds or repairs. The Children's Emergency Bureau was set up in Guernsey with a team of hard working women, darning, mending, knitting, making clothes and making do with whatever materials they could find. (Source 35) Elastic became non-existent and caused a problem with some items of underwear. The success of the allied landings in France brought even more shortages and hardship to the islands when they became cut off from the French ports.

Clothes were commandeered by the States from evacuated houses. Arrangements were made for payment to be credited to the owners after the war. Children's clothes were handed down or exchanged for larger or smaller sizes. Blankets were cut up to make warm winter coats (Source 36) and curtains and sheets and tablecloths were made into underwear, dresses and suits. Articles of clothing were patched and patched and patched again until the original garments were hardly recognisable. Emergency clothing and footwear sent by the British government at liberation, were welcomed with open arms.

MAKE DO AND MEND

As the occupation continued, tools, utensils, machinery and all kinds of other things wore out with no easy means by which to replace them. People had to improvise and many discovered skills they never knew they possessed.

Bicycles being the main form of transport required constant repair. When they were beyond it, the best parts were made into one machine or sometimes a tandem on which two people could ride. Tyres were a continuing problem and Green's Cycle Shop in Guernsey acquired a secondhand stitching machine from one of the shoe shops. With the help of a former boot repairer, the stitching machine and a large supply of leaky fire-hoses obtained from the Fire Station, Green's had sufficient tyre repairing materials to last through the occupation. Even so the demand for repairs was so great that many people throughout the islands had to replace worn tyres with garden or greenhouse hosepipes or ride on the rims. (Source 37) Inner tubes were repaired with patches cut from worn out inner tubes. When solution for sticking them together ran out in Guernsey a chemist found a formula for making some more.

Often supplies from France, such as bicycle tyres and needles for sewing machines, would be the wrong size, but usually someone managed to find a way of converting them. Strong needles for use on leather were made from wire. These were sharpened to a point at one end and flattened at the other with a hole drilled through it to carry the thread.

A variety of cooking utensils was made from empty tins by island tinsmiths and householders when no new metal could be obtained for repairs. Oil and paraffin lamps were also made from tins, with bootlaces or cord being dipped in candle grease for the wicks. In fact any fuel that could be obtained was used. As one islander said: 'It was a wonder we didn't blow ourselves up, because I used to nick a drop of German petrol out of horizontal petrol tanks and mix it with a thick oil that we had – and hope for the best! It gave quite a bit of light, but produced a terrible smoke.'

A typical sawdust stove was made from a large tin approximately 22 cms high with a diameter of approximately 18 cms. A small hole was cut in the base, large enough to insert the handle of a broom, to create an air passage through the tightly packed sawdust. Another air passage was formed through the top. (Source 19) There seemed to be no limit to the inventiveness and imagination of people. They made an enormous variety of useful items from any materials they could find. (Sources 38, 39 and 40)

FOOTWEAR

Leather was imported to the islands from France for the repair and manufacture of shoes. The States of Guernsey set up a boot factory which was operated by a staff of six and 700 pairs of working boots had been turned out by the beginning of 1942. Other better class shoes, including those for infants and children, were also made, using Guernsey hides tanned in France. (Source 42) As footwear became even harder to obtain (Source 43) many people made footwear from oddments around the home. (Source 41) Unfortunately shoes made from rope soles and knitted uppers and wooden soles with canvas uppers did not last very long. (Source 44)

The Summerland Factory in Jersey, which had been re-opened for the manufacture of clothes and knitwear also turned out footwear for Jersey and Guernsey. This gave valuable employment to over 250 people.

Sidney Farnworth, the son of a Lancashire clog maker, was put in charge of producing the wooden soled Jersey boot and shoe. Over 45,000 pairs were made under his supervision and thousands of repairs were also carried out. The wooden soles used up vast quantities of the local beech wood, 500 tons in all, which is to be regarded as an ecological misfortune at any time. So important was the work undertaken by Mr. Farnworth that, although he had been born in England, his job saved him from deportation to an internment camp in Germany.

Ordinary wooden soles tended to cause flat feet and constant foot exercises were needed to relieve the symptoms. People with foot trouble were able to obtain flexible wooden-soled shoes on the presentation of a medical certificate. These shoes had the added luxury of a strip of rubber fixed across a crack in the sole and were a lot more comfortable for walking.

In *War on Sark* Julia Tremayne wrote how Sybil Hathaway, the Dame of Sark, gave her some rug wool and little bits of leather to make shoes for the young children to change into when their feet were wet. She also wrote: 'I am soling my boots with those rubber mats that come off pub counters.'

TOBACCO

It is surprising to note the great importance people placed on cigarettes and tobacco at times during the occupation when food was so scarce. It is even more surprising to note that a pound of tobacco sold for £112 in 1945. Cigarettes and tobacco were rationed towards the end of 1940. The initial amount fixed for civilians over 18 years was either 20 cigarettes, five cigars, 10 cigarillos or two ounces of tobacco a week. A similar quantity, but with one ounce of tobacco, was fixed for members of the German forces per day! The weekly ration for civilians varied throughout the five years of occupation.

Tobacco in any form had a great barter value and the troops were happy to exchange it for food, clothes, and all kinds of other commodities, much of which they sent back to their families in Germany.

From 1941 civilians were permitted to grow the plants under licence. (Source 45) Many dried and cured the tobacco themselves (Source 46) crushing the leaves through an old mangle or putting them in a tobacco press. (Source 47) A simple machine (Source 48) was used to finely shred them. One islander described this tobacco as the 'scorched earth policy'. To breathe heavily or to cough when smoking it would send a shower of burning ash over clothes, carpets and soft furnishings.

To supplement dwindling rations, many islanders smoked dried bramble leaves, rose petals, cherry leaves, sweet chestnut leaves or clover, to name but a few. In fact if it would burn they smoked it, sometimes making themselves quite sick in the process. It was even said that some smoked the tea in their Red Cross parcels when these arrived towards the end of the occupation!

Tobacco leaves were sent to tobacco manufacturing companies in the islands and processed into neatly rolled cigarettes. They looked marvellous when they arrived back in their packets – but the taste left a lot to be desired, according to some smokers. On one occasion a Guernseyman bribed a German soldier with a packet of these cigarettes to let him take some stored wood for a fire. (Due to the scarcity of fuel it was illegal for islanders to cut down trees for firewood). He could not help thinking when he was safely back home that the soldier might wonder whether they had been worth the risk when he smoked them.

HEALTH

A poor diet affected the physical growth of children throughout the islands. The average height of 6 to 14 year olds in Jersey was reduced by about one and a half inches between 1940 and 1943, and the average weight was also down a few pounds in the same age groups.

In general children and people under the age of 40 were in reasonable health and teeth were good. Most problems occurred amongst the elderly and invalids. By the end of 1944 loss of weight generally was serious and the first consignment of International Red Cross parcels arrived just in time to prevent a real threat of starvation.

People who had been overweight lost pounds of unhealthy fat and many of them recovered from heart, lung and thyroid troubles. Unfortunately other people, particularly those among the elderly and some of the manual workers, became weak and quite a few died of malnutrition until the situation improved with the arrival of the Red Cross parcels.

According to the Ministry of Health in Whitehall, who issued a report after the war, malnutrition had not been widespread. The average daily intake of calories had largely been maintained at somewhere between 2,100 and 2,500 calories until July 1944, then by the end of the year had fallen below 1,625 calories and in Jersey 1,700. (Source 49) The average daily intake of calories for men should on average be about 3,000 and for woman 1,750 with minimum requirements being 2,000 for men

Food, Clothing and Daily Life

and 1,500 for women. The occupation figures, however, were based on people being able to supplement their basic rations from their own stocks of food, poultry, rabbits and the black market. People living in the town areas and those not dealing in the black market in general had to make do with basic rations. It was not unusual for people to queue for four hours for one parsnip and find none left when it came to their turn.

Vegetables	Calories	Average calorie values received from basic rations:	
2 lbs. Parsnips	508	Period Sept. - Mar.	Calories
1 lb. Swedes	145	1941-42	1,219.7
1 lb. Turnips	119	1942-43	1,473.4
1 lb. Cabbage	141	1943-44	1,335.6
8 ozs. Onions, Beets or carrots	**80**		
	993		

Source 49: These tables show how difficult it would have been to supplement the diet with the large amount of vegetables required to make up the calorie value, especially when vegetables were scarce.

Dysentery and other bowel disorders were common throughout the occupation. The diet and lack of soap also caused skin complaints such as scabies, eczema and impetigo. There were a large number of cases of tuberculosis, although frequently these were exaggerated, perhaps in order to obtain extra benefits from the Germans.

An outbreak of typhus amongst the forced labourers in Guernsey in 1942 claimed 30 lives. This was not surprising, considering the conditions under which they had to live. The rat-infested rooms where they slept were filthy and their bodies crawled with lice. In 1944 there were 277 cases of diphtheria in Jersey and 93 of these were adults. As a result all children were vaccinated and inoculated but there were insufficient drugs or vaccines to treat the disease properly. Hospitals were closed to visitors and dances were cancelled. Children under 14 years of age were banned from public meetings, parties and theatre performances. When there was no more fuel at least one ambulance remained mobile – drawn by two horses! (Source 50)

Medical supplies, always in short supply, were imported from France, with many life-threatening delays in their transport. Worse still crates and boxes were often rifled on the journey and the contents, particularly insulin, were sold on the black market in France. Many diabetics died as a result. Torn strips of sheets replaced bandages, and sphagnum moss, which has an absorbent quality, was found useful as a substitute for cotton wool. Permission had to be obtained from the *Feldkommandant* for its collection from restricted areas.

A visit to the doctor for the Sarkees had its problems. The local doctor had left with the evacuees before the occupation and Dr. Pittard, a retired doctor, had taken over the practice. Sadly he died in June 1942 and the islanders were obliged to attend the German medical officer of health. In order to visit a doctor in Guernsey they first had to see the German MOH so that he could ascertain that their request for a permit to travel was on genuine medical grounds.

EDUCATION

Many schools were closed down, partly because of the evacuation of children of school age with their teachers, but also due to buildings being turned into barracks for German troops. Often they were requisitioned at such short notice that there was little time to find alternative accommodation for the pupils. One school in Guernsey had to be re-housed in a chapel.

During winter months homework was often done in the poor light of a candle or a homemade oil lamp. Despite this and other difficulties the standard of education was generally good. In Guernsey a special school leaving examination was produced. (Source 51) Certificates issued locally were later recognised by the Oxford and Cambridge Examining Board. A similar examination was set up in Jersey, but certificates were not issued by the Joint Board in England until after the occupation when the marked papers were submitted to them.

German was first taught in schools on a voluntary basis, then made compulsory by January 1943. (Source 52) German civilians living in the islands were asked to give lessons. The Education Councils were concerned that children, already learning English and French, were now expected to take on a third language. The complaint went unheeded by the Germans, but the Dame of Sark, whose knowledge of German had stood her in good stead with the occupying forces, encouraged the children in Sark to learn the language. During the winter months, when it was too cold to use the unheated schoolroom, she allowed the children to gather in the comfort of her home, La Seigneurie.

Leaflets dropped over the islands by British planes (Source 22) were often found by children and taken to school, causing their teachers a great deal of worry. In the event of being caught by the Germans in possession of a copy, the culprits and their families were dealt with severely, usually receiving a prison sentence and a fine. It was not surprising, therefore, that when Mr. Peter Girard, headmaster of a school in Guernsey was requested to allow a German schoolmaster to sit in on lessons to improve his English, it caused Mr. Girard quite a headache. (Source 53) It got even bigger after he received a quiet warning from a member of the civil police that the German schoolmaster was a member of the Gestapo! (In actual fact it was the *Feldgendarmerie*, the German Military Police, and not the Gestapo.) Concerned that he had been placed there to spy on them, the school treated him with caution, which was just as well as, despite turning out to be very pleasant, he admitted to Mr. Girard in a letter many years later that he had indeed been placed there for that purpose. He assured him, however, that he had never made any bad report on the school.

RED CROSS PARCELS

For a short while after the event of D-Day on 6 June 1944, islanders were happy in the belief that freedom was in sight and that their misery would soon be over. What they did not know was that they were not to be liberated for nearly another year.

The success of the Allied invasion of France was responsible for cutting off supplies of desperately needed food and medicines. Germans and civilians alike now faced the risk of starvation to such an extent that, in order to conserve food for the garrison, the Germans considered the possibility of:-

(a) evacuating to Germany those civilians not involved in working on the land (a move which Hitler could have authorised while the shipping lines were still open);

(b) persuading the UK government to transport to England all civilians, other than men who could fight against Germany and who were needed to work on the land; and

(c) persuading the UK government to send food to the islands (in which event the Germans would be able to commandeer even more of what was left of the civilian food supplies).

In the first instance Hitler waited too long to make a decision about the civilian evacuation. Secondly there were lengthy arguments and discussions within the British War Cabinet about sending food to the islands on the basis that it would prolong the war. The threat of general starvation and the deterioration of health of the civilian population finally outweighed the risk.

Records show the following food situation which led up to an urgent request for Red Cross food parcels and supplies:-

10 August 1944: There was enough food to feed the German troops for up to three months. Hitler sent orders to the commanders of the Channel Islands that civilian food was to be ruthlessly cut back in order to supplement the garrison's dwindling rations. This order was in fact in breach of Article 52 of the Hague Convention.

15 September: Food for troops and civilians was expected to last 45 days.

19 September: The German Foreign Ministry stated inaccurately (in order to ensure that the occupying troops would be fed until the end of spring 1945), that civilian food supplies were exhausted. The British government was asked to evacuate a large number of civilians or to send in relief food.

27 September: The British Prime Minister resisted sending food, as he thought this would prolong the occupation. The decision not to evacuate civilians was taken because ships were not available for that purpose.

2 October: Stocks of medicines were exhausted. Soap, cereals, sugar, salt and tobacco needed to be replenished immediately.

13 October: A German press notice declared that they were no longer responsible for feeding the civilian population of the islands as a request had been made through the protecting power for relief food to be sent to the islands.

31 October: A German report recorded that the garrison's food was expected to last until May 1945, but that there would be nothing left for the civilians after January 1945.

Food, Clothing and Daily Life

7 November: A decision was taken by the British government to request the Red Cross to send food and medical supplies to the islands for the civilian population.

December: Rations were reduced to a minimum existence level. The estimated daily intake of calories was a third of those in the United Kingdom – approximately 1,137 compared with 3,500.

27 December: The SS *Vega* first arrived in Guernsey.

29 December: The SS *Vega* first arrived in Jersey.

Contents of New Zealand Red Cross Parcel		**Contents of Canadian Red Cross Parcel**	
Tea – 2 packets	3 ozs	Biscuits	20 ozs
Corned Mutton	19 ozs	Chocolate	6 ozs
Lamb/Green Peas	15 ozs	Sardines	5 ozs
Chocolate	8 ozs	Milk Powder	20 ozs
Butter	20 ozs	Prunes	6 ozs
Coffee & Milk	15 ozs	Salmon	10 ozs
Sugar	10 ozs	Corned Beef	14 ozs
Peas	9 ozs	Raisins	8 ozs
Jam	20 ozs	Sugar	8 ozs
Milk (condensed)	20 ozs	Tea	4 ozs
Cheese	15 ozs	Cheese	4 ozs
Raisins	6 ozs	Ham	13 ozs
		Jam	16 ozs
		Pepper and Salt	1 oz
		Soap	3 ozs

Source 55: Examples of contents in Red Cross Parcel.

Aspects of War

The Swedish ship, the SS *Vega* (Source 1) under charter to the International Red Cross, left Lisbon in Portugal, carrying 750 tons of stores and arrived in the Channel Islands on 27 December 1944.

It was the first of six trips. (The sixth trip was made in June 1945 after the liberation of the islands.) Her cargo included over 100,000 parcels, 4,700 invalid diet parcels, soap, salt, medical supplies, children's clothes and cigarettes. (Source 54) In all over the six trips she carried a total of 460,000 food parcels for the civilian population, mainly donated by Canada and New Zealand. (Source 55) Each parcel was intended to provide a person with 462 calories a day. It was not until the third trip, however, that the SS *Vega* brought much needed flour and yeast. During February the islands had been completely without bread for three weeks. The Red Cross bread and flour added 987 calories daily to the diet. (Sources 56 and 57)

And so with the promise of liberation in sight, the people of the Channel Islands prepared themselves to welcome the liberating forces and to await the moment of reunion with families and friends whom they had not seen for five seemingly endless years.

Food, Clothing and Daily Life

Source 1: The SS Vega built in 1913 at Gothenburg in Sweden, had a gross tonnage of 1,073. She was 226 feet 4 inches long with a 35 feet beam and a 14 feet 4 inches draft. Her speed was 9 knots. Photograph: *Carel Toms Collection, Priaulx Library*

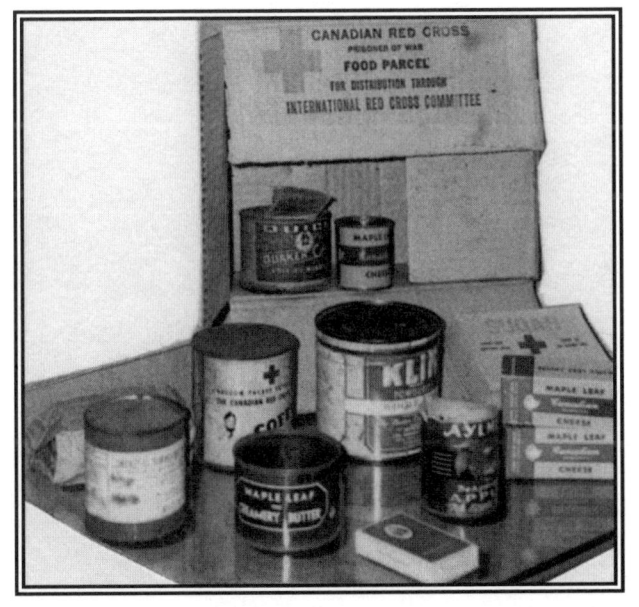

Source 2: A selection of food contained in a Red Cross Parcel. Refer to Source 55 for a full example of contents. *German Occupation Museum*

Source 3: States workers from Guernsey working in Alderney 1941. Photograph: *Carel Toms Collection*

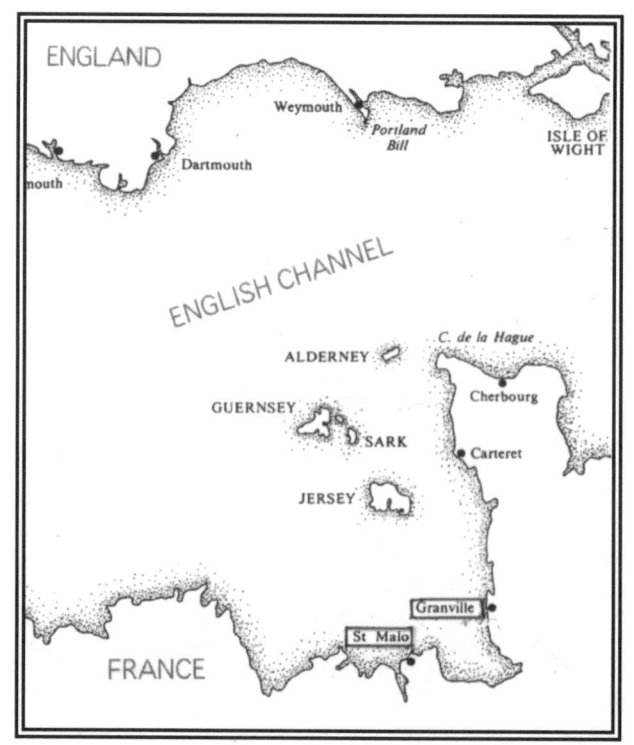

Source 4: Map showing locations of the purchasing commission in France.

Food, Clothing and Daily Life

Substitute foods photographed at the German Occupation Museum

Source 5: Parsnip coffee **Source 6:** Bramble tea

Source 7: Seawater salt **Source 8:** Carageen moss

Source 9: Potato flour

Source 10: Sugar beet press. *German Occupation Museum*

Source 11: Sugar beet (beta vugaria)

Source 12: Sugar beet press designed and made by Mr. J. T. Renouf, Jersey, from a wooden box, a wheel rim, two blocks of wood, a car jack handle. **Left:** the press dismantled.

Source 13: Bakers' oven in Jersey being filled with furze in preparation to cook food. Photograph: *Jersey Evening Post*

Food, Clothing and Daily Life

Source 14: An improvised oven made out of a biscuit tin. *German Occupation Museum*

Source 15: Metal stand used in hearths for cooking purposes. *Brooklands Farm, Guernsey*

Aspects of War

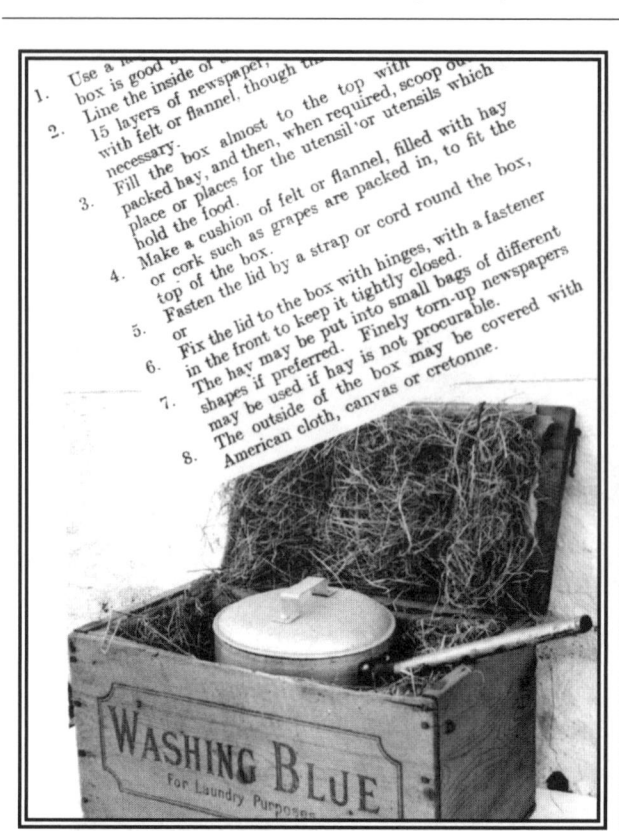

1. Use a [...]
   box is good [...]
2. Line the inside of [...]
   15 layers of newspaper, [...]
   with felt or flannel, though [...]
   necessary.
3. Fill the box almost to the top with [...]
   packed hay, and then, when required, scoop out [...]
   place or places for the utensil or utensils which [...]
   hold the food.
4. Make a cushion of felt or flannel, filled with hay [...]
   or cork such as grapes are packed in, to fit the [...]
   top of the box.
5. Fasten the lid by a strap or cord round the box, [...]
   or
6. Fix the lid to the box with hinges, with a fastener [...]
   in the front to keep it tightly closed.
7. The hay may be put into small bags of different [...]
   shapes if preferred. Finely torn-up newspapers [...]
   may be used if hay is not procurable.
8. The outside of the box may be covered with [...]
   American cloth, canvas or cretonne.

Source 18: Hay box made from wooden box and straw.
German Occupation Museum

Source 16: Extract from recip[e]
book, Hints of Wartime Cooker[y]
issued by the States of Guernse[y]
giving instructions on how [to]
construct a hay box.

HAY BOX COOKERY

A USEFUL TIME TABLE

Hay boxes are now in common use in the Island and are proving invaluable as savers of fuel.

Many persons do not get the full value owing to not heating the food on the fire after placing in a hay box, as well as before. This is a very important point.

The "Jersey Evening Post" recently had this very practical Time Table for hay box cookery:—

Dishes	Time on Fire	Time in Box
Lentil Soup	20 minutes	4 hours or overnight
Boiled Meat	20 "	4 hours or overnight
Stews	20 "	3 hours or overnight
Hot Pot	30 "	3 hours
Porridge	10 "	all night
Milk Pudding	5 "	3 hours
Fresh Fruit	3 "	1 "
Dried Fruit	10 "	2 "
Roly Poly Pudding (boiled in cloth)	20 "	3 "
Steamed Puddings	30 "	3 "

Housewives may wish to cut out this for reference.

Source 17: Guernsey Evening Pr[ess]
dated 5.1.42

Source 19: Sawdust stove whic[h]
was used for cooking purposes.
German Occupation Museum

Food, Clothing and Daily Life

Source 20: Fishing boats laid up at the Old Harbour, St. Peter Port, following the order for all boats to be moved to main harbours. Photograph: Carel Toms Collection

Source 21: The eight-foot dinghy in which Dennis Vibert escaped from Jersey to England in September 1941. Photograph: Carel Toms Collection

Source 22: Leaflet dropped by the RAF dated 30.9.1940 containing a report on the escape of a party of eight men from Guernsey.

ANORDNUNG FUER FISCHER

Hafenueberwachungsstelle, St. Peter-Port.

Ab sofort müssen alle Fischerboote, die von den Haefen von Guernsey und von Sark aus Fischfang betreiben, mit blau-weiss-roten senkrechten Streifen von je 10 Zoll Breite versehen werden und zwar an jeder Seite des Bugs hinter der Reg. Nr. rundherum und innerhalb des Bootes an von oben best sichtbarer Stelle. Diese Anordnung muss bis zum 10.7.42 befolgt sein.

ORDER FOR FISHERMEN

As from to-day all fishing boats, starting from the harbours of Guernsey and Sark for fishing purposes, must be furnished with blue-white-red stripes, each 10 inches wide. These stripes have to be painted vertically on each side of the bow all round the boat behind the Registered Number and inside the boat on the spot most conspicuous from above. The present Order has to be executed by July 10th.

Die Hafenueberwachungsstelle St. Peter-Port.

OBERMEYER,
Kapitaenleutnant und
Dienststellenleiter

Source 23: Notice printed in the Guernsey Evening Press dated 8.7.1940.

FISHING

NOTICE FROM THE GERMAN HARBOURKOMMANDANT.

We learn from the German Harbourkommandant that for all fishing from a boat with net, rod, line or pots, a permit from his office is necessary.

For low-water fishing along the coast, such as winkling, crabbing, prawning or sand-eeling, and rod fishing along the coast, no permit is required. This sort of fishing is not allowed in the vicinity of where guards of the German forces are stationed or the Town Harbours.

The time when fishing is allowed is from 6 a.m. till 8 p.m. for all fishermen.

Source 24: Jersey Evening Post dated 20.7.1940

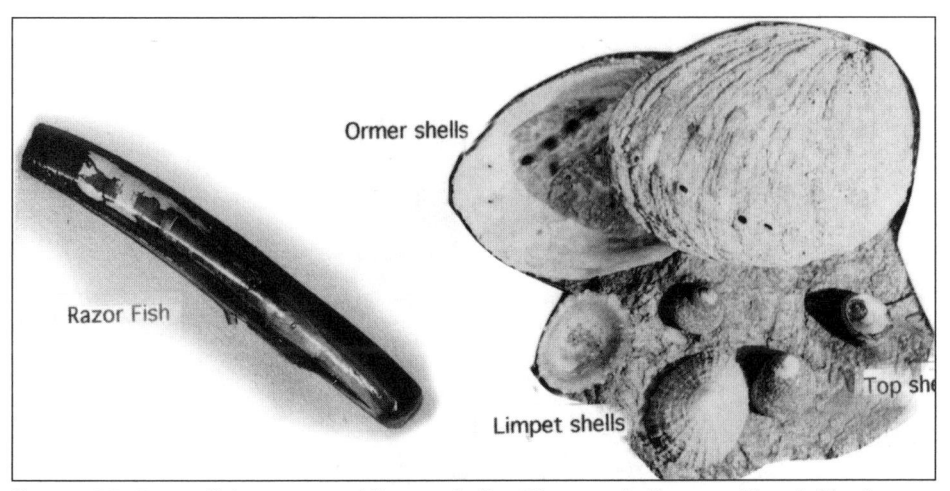

Source 25: Razor fish, ormer and limpet shells. The top shells resemble winkles but are smaller and inedible.

"BLACK MARKET"

FOUR GUERNSEYMEN SENTENCED IN JERSEY

The Military Tribunal of the Feldkommandantur 515 St. Helier, Jersey, had before them recently the case in which Guernseymen were charged with having been guilty during the period September to December, 1941, of purchasing in Guernsey four pigs, 15 cows and two young heifers without permit, and, after slaughtering them, selling the meat.

After hearing the evidence, the accused were found guilty of this charge, and the sentences were pronounced on Friday, January 16, as follows:—

Source 26: Extract from the Guernsey Evening Press dated 26.1.1942. As a warning to other would be offenders, a prison sentence of 12 months and a fine of RM3,000 Reichsmarks (£300) - were given to greenhouse labourer, an eight months sentence with a fine of RM2,000 (£200) and six months' sentence with a fine of RM1,400 (£140) to two growers respectively. The fourth man received a five months' sentence with RM1,200 fine (£120).

Source 27: Guernsey Evening Press dated 22.7.1942

NOTICE

PIGS

THE attention of farmers and others is again drawn to the Order, dated the 4th September, 1941, whereby:—

1. All pigs over six weeks of age have to be registered with the Farm Produce Board.
2. The Farm Produce Board must be notified of the proposed removal of such a pig from the premises where it is kept.
3. The Farm Produce Board must be notified when such a pig is slaughtered or dies.

It is imperative that this Order should be obeyed. The penalty for failure to do this is imprisonment for a term not exceeding two years or to a fine not exceeding £500 or to both such imprisonment and such fine.

For and on behalf of The Controlling Committee of the States of Guernsey.

R. O. FALLA,

Hirzel House,
Guernsey.
20th July, 1942.

(2168)

Food, Clothing and Daily Life

Source 28: Queue of people waiting to be served in St. Peter Port. Photograph: *Carel Toms Collection*

		GUERNSEY	
Average weekly ration prior to the Allied Invasion of France June 1944		Reduction in Average weekly ration February 1945	
Bread	4 lbs.10 ozs.	No bread 14th February to 8th March	
Meat (including bone)	3 ozs.or 4 ozs.	No meat	
Butter	2 or 4 ozs.	No butter	
Cooking fat	1 oz.	No cooking fat	
Flour or oats	6 ozs.	Oatmeal flour	1 oz.
*Skimmed milk	3 pts	Skimmed milk	2 pts.
*Potatoes	5 lbs.	Potatoes	5 lbs.
Suet	1 ozs.		
Sugar	3 ozs.or 4 ozs.		
Coffee Substitute	1 oz.		
Macaroni	1 1/2 ozs.		

*Rations in Jersey were of similar quantities, but potatoes were on average 7 lbs per week and full milk 5 1/2 pts per week. These two items were the mainstay of the Jersey diet.

Source 29: Comparison of weekly rations during the period prior to the allied invasion of France in 1944 and 8 months later.

Aspects of War

Source 30: Jersey Evening Post dated 1.2.1941

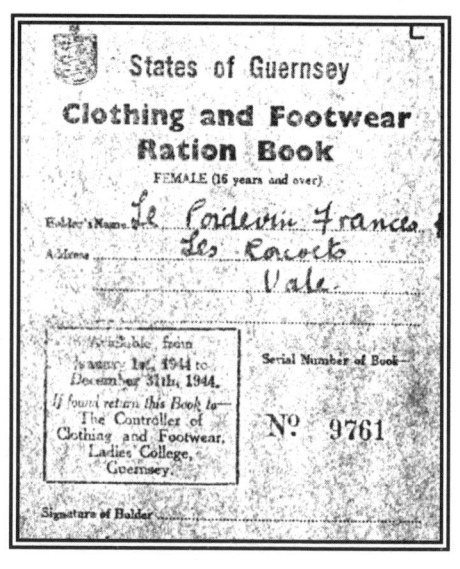

Source 31: A Guernsey clothing and footwear ration book. Similar books were issued in Jersey.

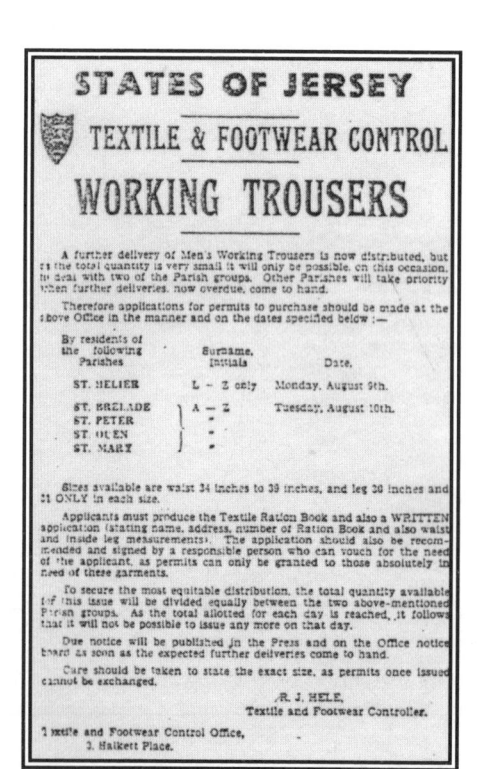

Source 32: Notice in the Jersey Evening Post regarding the allocation of working trousers.

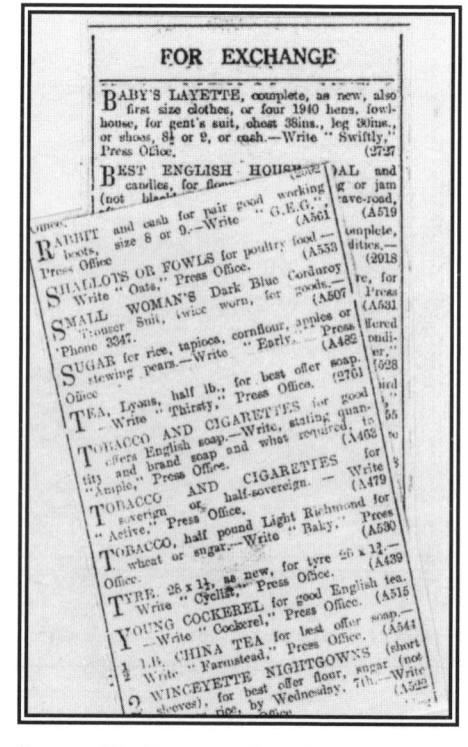

Source 33: Guernsey Evening Press dated 5.1.1942

EXCHANGE AND MART

EXCHANGE pair HEAVY BOOTS (size 8) for Shoes (size 8); also a pair Black Light Boots for Shoes (size 8). Write, "V.328," "Evening Post."

EXCHANGE. LADIES' FLAT-HEEL SHOES, or Wellingtons, or Gent's (7 or 8), for Sir Herbert Barker Shoes (size 9), wide fitting, or any other make. Phone 441.

Source 34: Jersey Evening Post dated 21.7.1941

THE CHILDREN'S EMERGENCY BUREAU

The Children's Emergency Bureau asks us to express their thanks to all sewers and knitters who have given so much of their time in helping them; also to all kind donors of parcels received, since they opened. It has been impossible to acknowledge them all. The communication continues:

"We wish them all a Happy New Year and hope that they will continue to help us. We have a work party at High Street every Wednesday from 2 to 4.30, for mending, darning, etc. All helpers will be welcome. We endeavour to provide baby clothes or any child's garment required. Our telephone number is 1414."

ALADDIN REPEATS WITH NEW NUMBERS

Source 35: Extract from the Guernsey Evening Press dated 7.1.1942

Food, Clothing and Daily Life

Source 36: Mrs. Jessie Baudains wearing a winter coat made for her during the Occupation out of an old army blanket.

Source 37: Bicycle with tyres replaced by garden or greenhouse hosepipe. Note the join in the hose between the front fork and the mudguard. German Occupation Museum

Source 38: Wooden chair made during the Occupation in wood taken from an Organisation Todt wood dump which was situated on the Circus Field in Jersey. The OT was a German civilian organisation formed before the war which arranged for military construction work to be undertaken by their German and foreign labour force.
Channel Islands Occupation Society, Jersey

Food, Clothing and Daily Life

Source 39: Stable broom with wire bristles and a smaller brush with bristles formed out of paper. German Occupation Museum

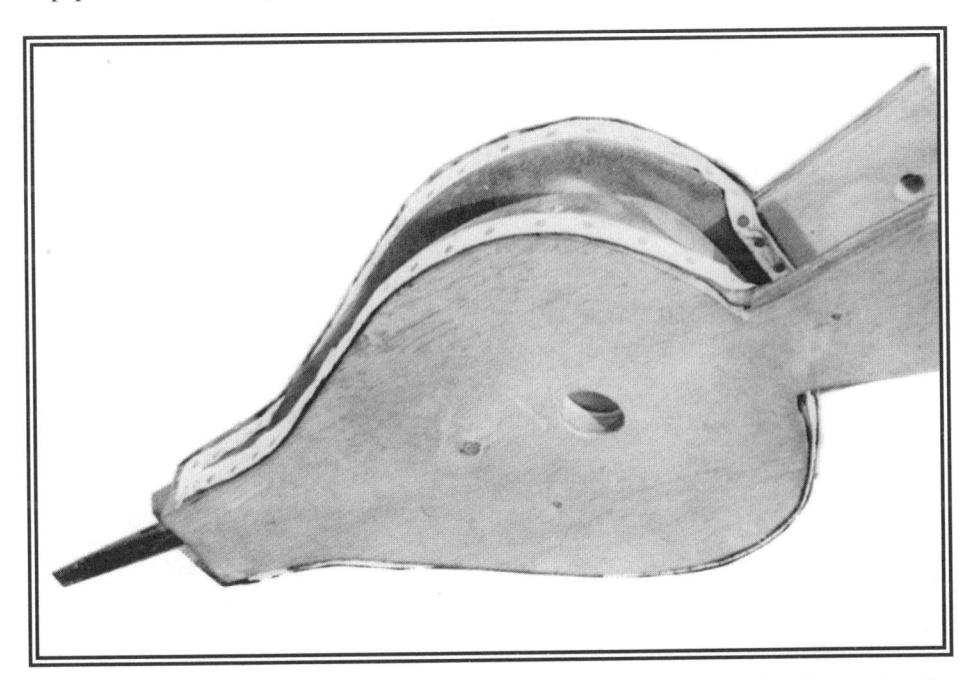

Source 40: A pair of fire bellows – typical of those made during the Occupation for blowing air onto a fire. Channel Islands Occupation Society, Jersey

Aspects of War

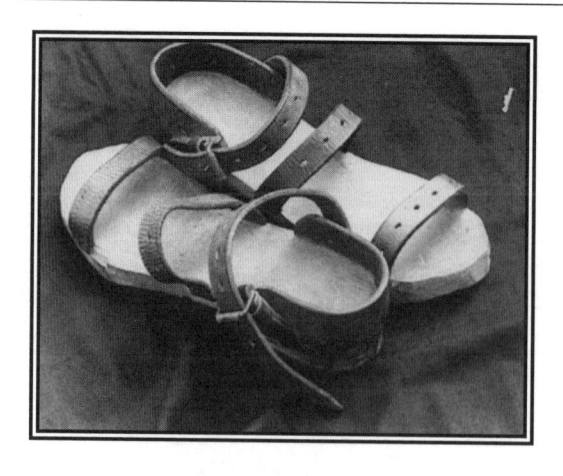

Source 41: Wooden soles sandals.
Photograph: Carel Toms Collection

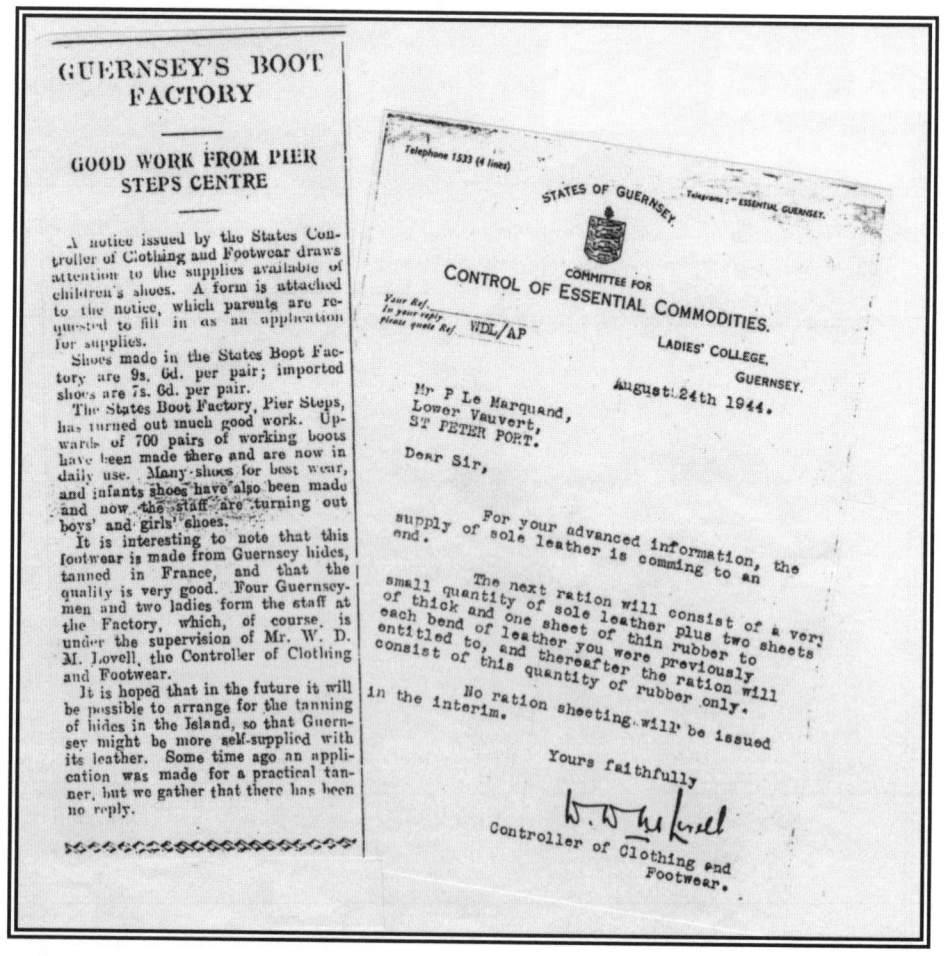

GUERNSEY'S BOOT FACTORY

GOOD WORK FROM PIER STEPS CENTRE

A notice issued by the States Controller of Clothing and Footwear draws attention to the supplies available of children's shoes. A form is attached to the notice, which parents are requested to fill in as an application for supplies.

Shoes made in the States Boot Factory are 9s. 6d. per pair; imported shoes are 7s. 6d. per pair.

The States Boot Factory, Pier Steps, has turned out much good work. Upwards of 700 pairs of working boots have been made there and are now in daily use. Many shoes for best wear, and infants shoes have also been made and now the staff are turning out boys' and girls' shoes.

It is interesting to note that this footwear is made from Guernsey hides, tanned in France, and that the quality is very good. Four Guernseymen and two ladies form the staff at the Factory, which, of course, is under the supervision of Mr. W. D. M. Lovell, the Controller of Clothing and Footwear.

It is hoped that in the future it will be possible to arrange for the tanning of hides in the Island, so that Guernsey might be more self-supplied with its leather. Some time ago an application was made for a practical tanner, but we gather that there has been no reply.

Telephone 1533 (4 lines)

STATES OF GUERNSEY

Telegrams: "ESSENTIAL GUERNSEY"

COMMITTEE FOR CONTROL OF ESSENTIAL COMMODITIES.

Your Ref
In your reply
please quote Ref. WDL/AP

LADIES' COLLEGE,
GUERNSEY.

August 24th 1944.

Mr P Le Marquand,
Lower Vauvert,
ST PETER PORT.

Dear Sir,

For your advanced information, the supply of sole leather is comming to an end.

The next ration will consist of a very small quantity of sole leather plus two sheets of thick and one sheet of thin rubber to each bend of leather you were previously entitled to, and thereafter the ration will consist of this quantity of rubber only.

No ration sheeting will be issued in the interim.

Yours faithfully

W. W. Lovell

Controller of Clothing and Footwear.

Source 42: Guernsey Evening Press dated 16.1.1942
Source 43: Letter from the States controller of clothing and footwear concerning the supply of shoe leather.

Food, Clothing and Daily Life

Source 44: Top: Knitted boots with rope soles. Bottom right: home-made canvas shoe with flexible wooden sole. Note base of sole in inset. Bottom left: Jersey shoe with wooden sole. Middle left: child's wooden soled sandals. *German Occupation Museum*

Source 45: Tobacco growing in Guernsey *Photograph: Carel Toms Collection*
Source 46: Dried tobacco leaves. *German Occupation Museum*

Source 47: Tobacco Press. *German Occupation Museum*

Source 48: Equipment for cutting home grown tobacco.
German Occupation Museum

Food, Clothing and Daily Life

Vegetables	Calories		Average calorie values received from basic rations:
2 lbs . Parsnips	508	Period Sept.-Mar.	Calories
1 lb. Swedes	145	1941-42	1,219.7
1 lb. Turnips	119	1942-43	1,473.4
1 lb. Cabbage	141	1943-44	1,335.6
8 ozs.. Onion, Beets or Carrots	80		
	993		

Source 49: These tables show how difficult it would have been to supplement the diet with the large amount of vegetables required to make up the calorie value, especially when vegetables were scarce.

Source 49: Included in body of text

Source 50: Horse drawn ambulance.
Photograph: Carel Toms Collection

STATES OF GUERNSEY

SCHOOL LEAVING CERTIFICATE EXAMINATION

As a result of an examination held in February, 1944, during the period of German Occupation, the Guernsey Education Council has awarded its School Leaving Certificate to _____ born on the 14th day of June in the year 1927 who satisfied the examiners as indicated below.

"Very Good" French (with oral)
Passed with Credit Mathematics
Passed Scripture
  English Language
  English Literature
  History
  Geography
  Elementary _____ (Suppl___)

E. Fossard
President,
States Intermediate
School Committee.

Jno. Rouxel
President

A. Winterflood
Secretary

Guernsey
Education
Council

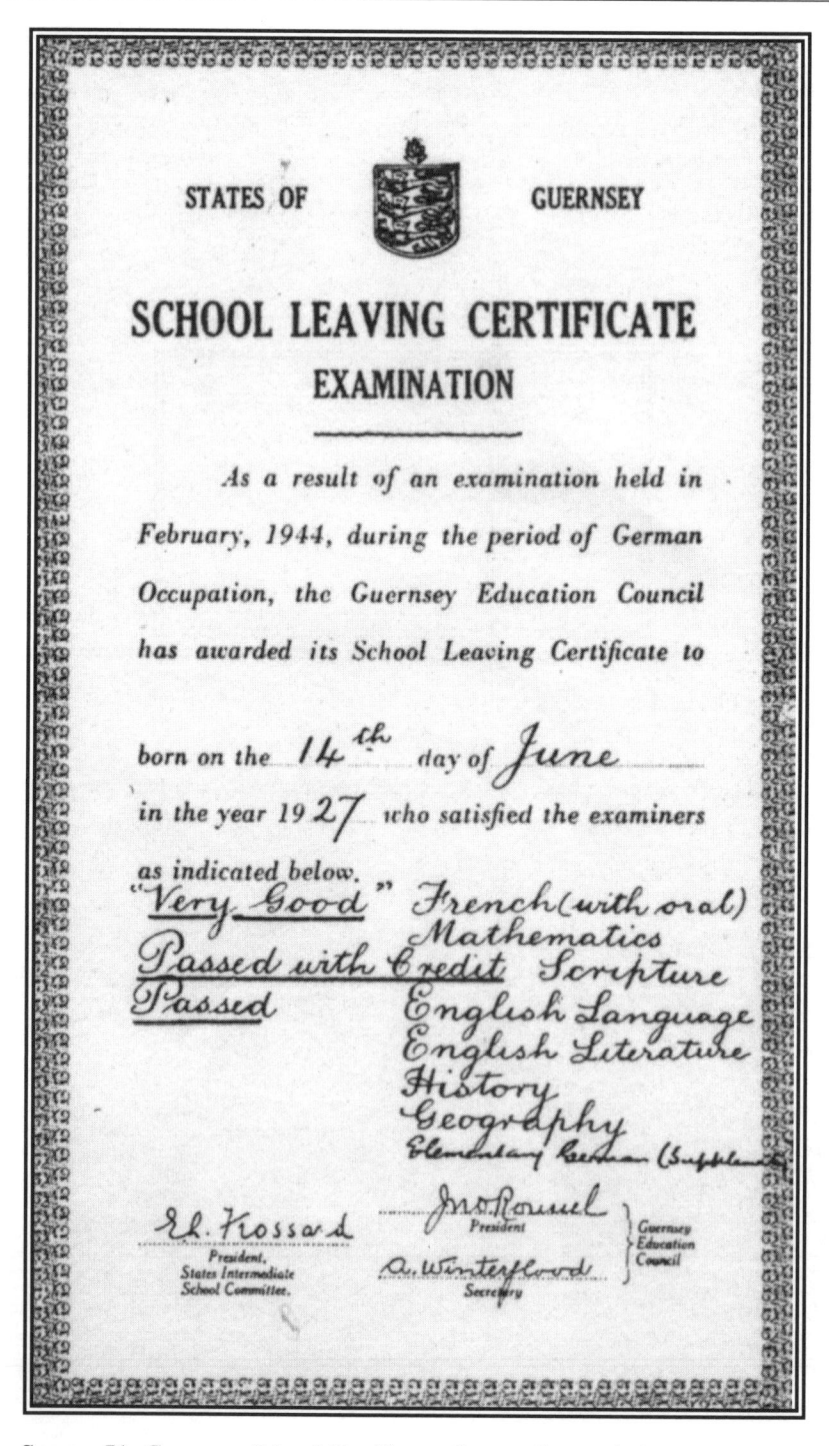

Source 51: Guernsey School Certificate, Occupation period.
P. J. Girard Collection

THE TEACHING OF GERMAN

PRIZE DISTRIBUTION AT EDUCATION OFFICE

An interesting ceremony was held at the States Education Office on Saturday morning when Jurat P. E. Brée, President of the Education Department, received Col. Knackfuss, Feld Commandant of the C.I., and other German officers, who had come for the purpose of presenting book prizes to teachers and pupils who had shown aptitude in teaching or acquiring a knowledge of the German language.

There was an attendance of about sixty, including headmasters and headmistresses, teachers of German, and the successful scholars.

Col. Knackfuss first thanked the teachers for the good work they had done and emphasised that the knowledge of German among the school-children has much improved. This was undoubtedly due to the good work done in the schools; he had personally visited several of the schools and was convinced that the children were interested and keen on extending their knowledge of German. He was, therefore, very pleased to present the prizes which had been placed at his disposal by the Militaer Befehlshaber.

Sonderfuehrer Bleul, Officer in charge of Education and Culture, then addressed those present. He stressed the importance of a knowledge of languages in general and of German in particular, pointing out that the German language is the most important on the Continent of Europe, being spoken by more than 100,000,000 and understood by another 50,000,000. He told his audience how, in Germany in 1940, that is after the war already on, English was the first foreign language in the education scheme of that country. He was sure that in Jersey there were many persons, both adults and young scholars, who welcome the opportunity which was now presented to them of acquiring a good knowledge of German. Even now, in war-time, Shakespeare was being played in Germany, in fact there were more performances there than in the land of his birth.

The recipients individually briefly expressed their thanks, and this brought the ceremony to an end.

Source 52: Jersey Evening Post dated 17.2.1944

Source 53: The German schoolmaster with some of the children of the Castel School, Guernsey. He later taught German to more advanced pupils.
Photograph: P. J. Girard Collection

Source 54: Unloading Red Cross parcels aboard the SS Vega.
Photograph: Author's Collection

Contents of New Zealand Red Cross Parcel		Contents of Canadian Red Cross Parcel	
Tea - 2 packets	3 ozs.	Biscuits	20 ozs.
Corned Mutton	19 ozs.	Chocolate	6 ozs.
Lamb/Green Peas	15 ozs.	Sardines	5 ozs.
Chocolate	8 ozs.	Milk Powder	20 ozs.
Butter	20 ozs	Prunes	6 ozs.
Coffee & Milk	15 ozs.	Salmon	10 ozs.
Sugar	10 ozs.	Corned Beef	14 ozs.
Peas	9 ozs.	Raisins	8 ozs.
Jam	20 ozs.	Sugar	8 ozs.
Milk (condensed)	20 ozs.	Tea	4 ozs.
Cheese	15 ozs.	Cheese	4 ozs.
Raisins	6 ozs.	Ham	13 ozs
		Jam	16 ozs.
		Pepper & Salt	1 ozs.
		Soap	3 ozs.

Source 55: Examples of contents in Red Cross Parcels delivered to the Islands

Source 55: included in body of text.

Aspects of War

Source 56: Collecting Red Cross parcels in St. Helier, Jersey.
Photograph: Jersey Evening Post

Source 57: Collecting Red Cross parcels in St. Peter Port, Guernsey.
Photograph: Carel Toms Collection

PART III
DAILY LIFE
AND LIBERATION

Transport
Fuel

Communications:
Newspapers
Resistance News Sheets
Radios
Red Cross Letters

Deportations
Internment Camps
Liberation

Transport in Guernsey and Jersey was a major problem for the civilian population throughout the German occupation. The use of cars for private purposes was forbidden and driving permits were granted for essential services only. The people of Sark did not have the same difficulties. There was no great distance to travel on the small island of 3.2 square kilometres. Horse-drawn vehicles and bicycles were the two established forms of transport there.

In September 1940 a German purchasing commission began to requisition large numbers of the islands' motor vehicles, a great many of which were sent to France. These were assessed by States-appointed valuers under the supervision of German valuers, and paid for at the time of purchase. (Source 1)

Early in 1941 an increase in the shortage of fuel forced the small number of doctors remaining in Guernsey after the evacuation to exchange their cars for motorcycles. It was quite an experience for some of them who had never previously ridden one. These machines were kept in running order throughout the occupation by a local dealer. Spare parts were not easy to obtain. On one occasion an enterprising dealer had a piston cast at the Town Foundry from a piece of aluminium. It was then turned to size and shape on a lathe in his workshop. The job was completed by making piston rings out of a cast-iron drainpipe.

Civil transport organisations were set up in Guernsey and Jersey. They were responsible for the allocation of a limited number of vehicles to various States departments and emergency services. In the early days of the occupation, some families had been ordered to leave their homes by Germans requiring the use of the accommodation for themselves. There was no transport available to move heavy goods and nowhere else allocated for them to live.

One Guernsey family, forced out of their home so that the Germans could set up a radio station on the top of their house (Source 2), had to transport a disabled member of the family in a wheelbarrow.

Later, when housing authorities were set up to liaise with the German authorities, people were re-housed and transport was provided for that purpose.

The petrol shortage increased and the German military authorities put greater restrictions on the use of motorised transport. Buses, vans, cars and lorries were converted to operate on gas, using portable equipment attached to the outside of the vehicle. (Source 3) In June 1941

Guernsey had 17 of these vehicles in use and a further 54 awaiting conversion. Jersey had only four buses and one taxi at that time, but later there was a substantial increase in number.

Charcoal, used to make the gas which drove the engines, tended to crumble into dust in transport. In 1943 it was replaced by wood and anthracite. (Charles Cruikshank gives a description of how vehicles operate on gas in *The German Occupation of the Channel Islands*, page 126.)

Bicycles were highly valued. All existing stocks with the dealers were quickly bought up within a week or two of the German restrictions on transport. Green's Cycle Shop in Guernsey sold their entire stock of 400 cycles in this short period. Dealers searched the quarries for old bicycle frames, wheels and other spare parts that had been scrapped before the invasion. Islanders were desperate for transport. Many broken-down machines were brought out for repair.

In 1942 the Germans requisitioned bicycles under Article 53 of the Hague Convention. (Source 4) Strong protests from the islands' authorities and appeals from islanders were ignored. In Jersey it was necessary to call up 3,200 cycles before 50 could be found in a suitable condition to make up the requisition order. The rest were in bad condition or needed for essential work. Guernsey faced similar problems in obtaining 150 to fill their quota.

Horse-drawn bus services operated for a time in the two larger islands, mainly in the town areas. (Source 5) Ambulances were also converted, and horse-drawn carts were used for moving furniture and other goods. (Source 6) A Guernsey farmer even managed to train a pair of bullocks to pull a cart to the market in St. Peter Port.

The Germans imported horses into the islands to be used in transport. (Source 7) Other fine horses were brought in to be ridden by the military. (Source 9)

When Hitler gave the order for fortification of the Channel Islands in October 1941 it soon became clear that railway systems would be required to move vast amounts of construction material needed for this operation. Much of the material was imported but large amounts of stone were obtained from the islands' quarries and sand from the beaches.

Railways had been in operation in the islands at one time but were no longer in existence at the start of the occupation. The German-built light railways were constructed by slave and forced labourers under

Organisation Todt. (Source 8) This organisation had been formed in 1933 by Dr. Fritz Todt, a civil engineer, who had undertaken civilian construction work in Germany using civilian workers. The large labour force needed to carry out Hitler's military requirements began to arrive in the islands in 1941. It included political prisoners and prisoners of war such as Russians, Spaniards, Poles, half-Jews and anyone who had offended the German authorities, as well as conscripted Dutch, Belgian, French and other workers.

In Guernsey the railway started in St. Peter Port and ended at L'Eree. The railway lines were laid without consideration to the population along roads, across fields and through private property. Steam locomotives burnt briquettes of coal or anthracite dust bound together by pitch or hard tar. Although it appears parts of the railway may have been dismantled after it had served its purpose, the section between St. Peter Port and St. Sampson remained in place until after liberation.

In Jersey a light railway track ran from St. Helier to Corbière, where it connected with another linking the Ronez quarry. Another line went from St. Helier to Gorey and another serviced the west coast from Western Quarries to La Pulente. The first railway was opened on 15 July 1942 with great pomp and glory and, according to Sinel's diary, *(The German Occupation of Jersey)* to a great deal of amusement on the part of the islanders. In all almost two-thirds of the coastline of both islands was covered by the railways. A small railway system, about 2.7 kilometres long, was also laid on Alderney. It was used to carry stone from the quarries to the fortification points.

Elsewhere in the islands Organisation Todt workers were used to construct concrete defence fortifications and the two underground hospitals on Guernsey and Jersey. Many of the forced labourers and slave labourers died during these constructions due to the extremely poor and dangerous conditions as well as the brutal treatment they received.

St. Lawrence Tunnels were started in 1941, with the construction originally designed to be used as an artillery barracks and a store for ammunition and later turned into an underground hospital when, following D-Day, an operating theatre, a dispensary and medical storerooms were added along with nurses' and doctors' quarters.

In Guernsey the German Military Underground Hospital in St. Andrews was used for approximately six weeks after the Normandy landings. It was made up of an operating theatre, dispensary, laboratory and x-ray facilities. It also provided staff sleeping quarters, a store room, mortuary and cinema.

In both islands the German authorities had previously taken over a civilian hospital for their wounded.

FUEL

Electricity, Gas and Wood:
Rationing of electricity and gas and the restriction of supplies varied between the islands but was started in Guernsey in July 1940 and in Jersey in October 1941. When households exceeded the ration, supplies were cut off as a penalty.

Before the Germans arrived coal was shipped from Newcastle and South Wales and petrol and oil from Southampton. With these supplies cut off the islands became dependent on France. Shipments of house coal, coke, briquettes and anthracite dust were few and not enough to cope with demand. Rations were based on the number of people in each household and the shortage of fuel caused serious difficulties and hardship. When there was none to be used for heating, the only way people could keep warm in many cases was to remain in bed.

From August 1941 in Jersey and November of the same year in Guernsey the gas service was limited to set hours morning and evening. Gas appliances were withdrawn or heavily restricted. Sinel notes in his diary that there was a number of gas poisoning accidents caused through people not turning off taps when the supply was stopped. They were gassed when it was re-started.

Similar restrictions on electricity came into effect from April 1942. The closure of the French ports in June 1944 after the Normandy landings meant that coal supplies came to an end in September. After gas supplies ceased in December 1944 and electricity in February 1945 households were forced to rely on their meagre rations of wood. (Source 15) The situation became so bad that cooking in community ovens came to an end, and restaurants closed in April 1945.

Because of the small size of the islands wood resources were limited. Wood fuel had been unrationed until July 1941, but from the beginning the German authorities had banned cutting down any tree or shrub without permission. Gathering wood could be done only with permission, even by owners and occupiers of property with timber.

The Germans were afraid too that felling too many trees around their military installations would expose them to aerial attacks.

People became desperate. They chopped up floorboards, doors, wooden fences and anything else that would burn. Wooden railway sleepers disappeared overnight. Civilians were prosecuted for stealing timber from greenhouses and any other structures. The Germans too were desperate for wood. There were instances when fine old furniture and even whole staircases were removed from houses to be used for kindling wood. When the French ports were closed in June 1944 household fuel was reduced to wood only. As an example the ration in Guernsey in December 1944 was:

Households of:	
1 person without gas or electricity for cooking	1 cwt. Wood
2 to 6	2 cwt. Wood
7 or more	3 cwt. Wood
1 person with gas or electricity for cooking	Nil
2 to 4	Nil
5 or more	Nil
Persons age 75 or over, medical reasons	Nil**
Babies under 18 months of age	1 cwt. Wood

(** covered by an emergency ration of other fuel.)

Source 10: States of Guernsey Report on Essential Supplies and Services during the occupation.

Peat:
During September 1940 cutting peat for fuel was begun in Jersey at St. Ouen's Bay and Grouville and in Guernsey at Vazon Bay. (Source 11) After it was cut the peat was neatly stacked to dry. Some time later it was used to help eke out other fuel.

Paraffin:
At no time was paraffin allowed to be used for cooking. It was issued to those households without gas or electricity for lighting. In July 1944 supplies were withdrawn, but hospitals and the fire brigade were exempt as they had to have an alternative form of lighting when electricity was cut off at night.

Sawdust and Tar:

A mixture of sawdust and tar was used as fuel in sawdust stoves. Food cooked on them could then be transferred to a hay box to finish cooking. (See Source 18 under Food, Clothing and Daily Life).

Candles:

Candles were scarce. Households without gas or electricity supplies were rationed to two and sometimes only one per week.

Petrol:

Petrol rationing was introduced in the islands before the occupation. The arrival of the German occupying forces brought further reductions.

The total number of cars in the Bailiwick of Guernsey in May 1940 was 5,465. The following table shows the drop in the number of civilian cars on the arrival of the Germans, and the civilian consumption of petrol per month over the five years.

Period	Cars	Petrol(gals)	Petrol(litres)
		(Consumption over month)	
May 1940	5,465	108,000	490,968
Aug 1940	445	17,258	78,455
Nov 1941) No. of vehicles reduced		6,600	30,000
Aug 1944) further by the Germans		4,400	20,000
Oct 1944) Civilian stock of petrol exhausted			
May 1945) so supplies allocated from German military stock		1,872	8,500

COMMUNICATIONS
Newspapers:
The German military authority went to great trouble to keep islanders ignorant of the true facts about how the war was progressing. German press officers were appointed to censor the newspapers in Jersey and Guernsey. (Source 12) Each item was carefully scanned to make sure that there was nothing offensive in it to the Third Reich. On one occasion in Jersey a newspaper run of 10,000 copies was completely scrapped since the press officer had missed an 'unacceptable' word in an advertisement.

Reports covering the war were supplied by German censors from their own news agencies. Many of them and other articles and notices were full of propaganda composed in such a way to trick the reader into believing they had been written by the editorial staff. In an effort to quietly expose this deception the editors left any bad grammar uncorrected. Where possible an odd word or two was slipped into the text to twist the meaning. Sinel's diary dated 28.1.41 notes: 'The German censor complains to the 'E.P.' (*Jersey Evening Post*) about the bad English that is allowed to pass in the Germans news.' Indeed, it is clear from the various diaries kept during the Occupation that the civil population did not believe everything they read.

The *Jersey Evening Post* and *Les Chroniques de Jersey* (the latter printed in French) were at first the only two newspapers in the island during the Occupation. The *Morning News* had ceased publication on the arrival of the Germans, although it was published again after the war for a short period. It is amusing to note that the Germans sent *Les Chroniques de Jersey* to Paris to be translated since part of it was printed in Jersey Norman-French, but the Parisians were also unable to understand it.

Deutsche Inselzeitung was introduced into Jersey for the German troops in 1940. It was first printed on the premises of the *Jersey Evening Post* and appeared on the front page of the paper. It was later issued as a single news sheet. A similar paper, called *Deutsche Guernsey Zeitung*, was published in Guernsey in 1942, using the premises of the *Guernsey Evening Press*.

The Germans had at first recommended an amalgamation of the *Guernsey Evening Press* and the *Guernsey Star*. This did not take place, but the two papers eventually agreed to print on alternate days throughout the week to conserve paper. (Source 13) In Jersey the *Post*, the only newspaper printed in English in that island, economised on paper by not publishing on a Thursday.

Over the five years of occupation the papers dropped in size from four pages to two and finally dwindled to one. At times publication had to be suspended when no paper was available. During these periods official announcements were displayed daily in the windows of the newspaper offices concerned.

Postal Service:
When supplies of one penny postage stamps ran out, the two penny stamps were cut in half diagonally. Eventually stamps were printed in the islands.

Telephone:
The public telephone service was suspended on and after D-Day in 1944. This created serious problems in cases of sudden illness particularly at night, and in isolated areas when curfew made it illegal to go out of doors to get help. Emergency services were seriously affected, even when partial services were restored to operate between 8 am and 8 pm. In January 1945 the service was cut off altogether until the end of the occupation.

When liberation came the telephone companies appealed for the return of earpieces which had been taken from public telephone boxes for use with illegal crystal sets. Many of them in fact were returned. (Source 14)

Resistance News Sheets:
Active resistance such as sabotage or helping escaped prisoners brought threats of swift reprisals, and even the death penalty. Escape from the islands was extremely dangerous and dependent on obtaining a boat to cross the Channel. Around 80 people from Jersey and 78 from Guernsey were successful over the five years. Others drowned in the attempt or had to turn back. A small number of young men in Jersey attempted to form a resistance group in 1944 but were given no encouragement to set it up. Disappointed at their failure, eight of them set about escaping to join the British forces. Five were successful, but three had to give up. Passive resistance, however, was carried out at every opportunity.

One such form was resistance news sheets. Charles Machon, a 51-year-old linotype operator at *The Star*, together with Cecil Duquemin, Ernest Legg, Francis (Frank) Falla and Joseph (Joe) Gillingham, formed the Guernsey Underground News Service (GUNS) in May 1942. (Source 16)   News was taken down illegally from the

BBC and typed up on thin tomato packing paper (see *The Silent War* by Frank Falla, pages 95 to 111 for the full story).

The news sheet had a circulation of about 300 until 11 February 1944, the date on which Charles Machon was betrayed by an Irishman he had thought to be reliable.

A large number of Irish seasonal labourers were in the islands when the Germans arrived. 450 were in Jersey alone, working on potato crops. As the Republic of Ireland was neutral, the Germans found the Irish a useful work force who were not restricted by the fact they were contributing to the German war effort. The rest of the population were exempt from military work under the Hague Convention.

Hubert Lanyon, a baker, and Wakley, a carrier, were the receivers of three copies of GUNS in Sark. These were read by more than 70 people in the island, including even a few trusted Germans. Following the arrest and interrogation of Charles Machon, Hubert Lanyon was also arrested. Despite a brutal interrogation Lanyon insisted that he had been the only person involved in receiving the news sheet in Sark. He was sentenced to six months imprisonment in Guernsey. It was later reduced to four months on appeal. He was more fortunate than the other GUNS publishers. All five were sent to Germany. Charles Machon, who suffered from severe stomach ulcers, died shortly afterwards. Joe Gillingham died while in prison. He had served his full sentence but his German gaolers refused to let him go.

In Jersey Herbert and George Gallichan produced a news sheet in June 1942 called the Bulletin of British Patriots, No. 1. This edition urged people not to give up their radio sets and pointed out that the Germans had no right to confiscate them under the Hague Convention. (Article 53 of the Hague Convention gave the Germans the right to remove transmitters, but it did not give them the right to remove wireless receivers.)

Unfortunately copies of the leaflets fell into the hands of the Germans. As a reprisal for its publication and a recent act of sabotage to telephone lines, the Germans arrested ten Jerseymen and held them hostage. This was followed by a threat that, if the true culprits did not come forward, these men would be deported to Germany. Furthermore, any other acts of sabotage would result in 20 more men being arrested and deported. The two brothers surrendered themselves, were court-martialled and imprisoned. George spent a year in Dijon prison and

Herbert spent the rest of the war in Wolfenbüttel concentration camp. Meanwhile the ten hostages were released.

Despite these events people continued to carry transcripts of the news with them or to pass it on verbally. There was always the danger that they might be betrayed by a collaborator or by someone seeking revenge. If caught they suffered the penalty of a heavy fine or imprisonment. Depending on the extent of their 'crime' some were sent to Germany. One such man was Canon Clifford Cohu in Jersey. He listened to the news on a hidden radio and passed it on to patients he visited in the hospitals. He, together with Joseph Tierney, a cemetery worker, and John Nicolle, the son of a farmer, were betrayed and arrested. All three were sent to Germany where they died.

Another news service, however, which did operate successfully was in Guernsey. Mr. L. E. Bertrand ran a news service without discovery from the confiscation of wireless sets in June 1942 until the liberation of the islands. He was assisted with the printing by Reg Warley, who worked at the Fruit Export depot. Although Mr. Bertrand was fortunate not to get caught, he did have a few narrow escapes. On one occasion he was protected from a French informer by a Polish friend. It seemed he threatened to kill the Frenchman if he gave Mr. Bertrand away and Mr. Bertrand heard no more about it.

Radios:

Radios were twice withdrawn throughout the islands by the Germans. (Source 15) The first occasion was for a short period at the end of 1940 as a punishment for help given by a number of islanders to British agents landing secretly in Guernsey. After the return of the sets they were confiscated on a small scale from people living in the immediate areas where 'V' signs had been painted or other forms of sabotage had been carried out. As a further punishment men between the ages of 18 and 55 were put on nightly two-hour patrols of a two-kilometre radius from the points involved.

The second time sets were withdrawn was in June 1942 until the end of the occupation, although the Irish neutrals were exempt from this order. The Germans gave the reason for confiscation as a military precaution. The BBC had been encouraging listeners in France and other occupied areas to take part in a general resistance campaign. This immediately brought an order from Berlin for the sets to be withdrawn.

An idea of the size of the operation can be gained from the 8,000 sets collected in Guernsey alone.

Despite an assurance that sets would eventually be returned to the owners, quite a large number were taken by the troops for their personal use. Many more were shipped to the continent.

In defiance of the order many people managed to hide wireless sets beneath floorboards, behind cupboards, inside armchairs, barrels and any other unlikely place they could think of. Being in possession of a crystal set or a radio was always dangerous. Houses were searched without warning. Some people were lucky enough to get away with it and some had narrow escapes. Presence of mind often saved the day. One desperate lady dropped hers in a saucepan of soup, while another carried a small set around under a tea cosy until the unwelcome visitors had gone. Many others were caught. The unfortunate ones were heavily fined or sentenced to imprisonment. Those with short sentences stayed in the islands. Others with longer sentences were sent to Germany where some of them died.

After the confiscation of their radios many people turned to making or acquiring crystal sets. Harry Capper fixed hundreds of crystal sets right under the noses of the *Feldgendarmerie*. His 'underground' repair depot in Guernsey was in the house occupied by them.

Red Cross Letters:
Red Cross messages to and from the Channel Islands were to provide a vital link between relatives and friends for the five years of occupation. They were brief and infrequent and usually took a minimum of three months to reach their destination via Europe. (Source 17)

A small number of messages trickled through during December 1940. The first large batch of letters did not arrive in the islands until the beginning of January 1941, seven months after the Germans had arrived. The Red Cross message bureau in Guernsey and the Bailiff's enquiry and news service in Jersey were set up to deal with these. Replies were originally restricted to ten words but later the number was increased to 25. (Source 19)

At the start of the service the bureau in Guernsey sent advice cards to addresses, requesting them to call at their premises. In Jersey messages were printed in the *Evening Post*. Later all messages were delivered through the islands' postal services.

Messages were strictly censored by the Germans and British.

Any part of the contents that might be interpreted as giving information of a military nature was banned. By February 1943 the number of messages which had been dealt with in Guernsey alone was more than 300,000. Jersey had dealt with in excess of 563,000 by the beginning of September 1944.

The islands' newspaper columns were regularly crammed with messages from relatives and friends (Source 17) until the publication of one in Guernsey which had been overlooked by the censor. It was from a headmaster who had been evacuated to the UK and was addressed to the Secretary of the Education Council. It read: 'All children very fit. Tommy, Joe and Sam's boys working hard. Doing very good work. Should graduate with honours near future. Delighting parents.' It was obvious that the boys' names represented Britain, Russia and America.

British censorship instruction for replies to messages included:
(1) Do not mention or hint about service matters. Even such remarks as 'Tom in Army', 'Jack gone East', 'Bill near where we spent holiday in 1938', etc., will not be passed by the censor.
(2) Do not mention the receipt of 'Radio Messages', 'Letters', or 'Cards'. Some non-committal phrase such as 'Received your message or news' should be used.
(3) Do not mention results of enemy action.
(4) Do not mention names of towns.
(5) Do not suggest corresponding through an intermediary or any means other than through the Red Cross.
(6) Do not cross out anything that you write on the form.

DEPORTATIONS
'In case of peaceful surrender the lives, property and liberty of peaceful inhabitants are solemnly guaranteed.'

These words were contained in the German demand for surrender on 1 July, 1940. With complete disregard to this promise a German order for the deportation of British subjects was printed in the Jersey and Guernsey newspapers on 15 and 16 September 1942, respectively. (Source 18)

The notice read: 'By order of Higher Authorities the following

British subjects will be evacuated and transferred to Germany:
   (a) Persons who have their permanent residence not on the Channel Islands, for instance those who have been caught here by the outbreak of war.
   (b) all those men not born on the Channel Islands and 16 to 70 years of age who belong to the English people, together with their families.'

More than 2,000 English-born residents and their families were deported to camps in Germany, Austria and France between September 1942 and February 1943, about four per cent of the total civilian population of the islands.

Hitler's purpose for the deportations was a reprisal for the decision of the British government in the autumn of 1941 to intern a large number of Germans in Iran who had been working against Britain and her allies. As soon as he became aware of these plans, Hitler threatened to hold hostage the English-born population in the Channel Islands. For every German interned in Iran, ten British civilians would be deported to the Pripet Marshes, a combat area in Poland. The British went ahead with the plan and it was thought that the final figure might reach 500.

The island authorities were ordered to draw up lists in the categories set out in the notice of 15 September 1942. (Source 18) The information was extracted from records compiled from October 1940 onwards for the purpose of identity cards, as directed by the Germans (see appendix). No further action was taken at this date as the Germans hoped to make an exchange of interned civilians. The following period of confusion between the Wehrmacht (German armed forces), and the German Foreign Ministry about the processing of Hitler's deportation order was responsible for it being overlooked until September 1942.

At the beginning of that month the Swiss government suggested an exchange of seriously wounded prisoners of war. The Channel Islands were included in the proposals. It was then that Hitler discovered his deportation order had never been carried out.

On 15 September 1942, a year after the original order had been issued, the Bailiff of Jersey, Alexander Coutanche (later Lord Coutanche) and the island Constables were called to a meeting by the *Feldkommandant.* They were informed that all British subjects who did not have their permanent residence on the Channel Islands (for instance

Aspects of War

people who had been prevented from returning to their homes on the mainland by the arrival of the occupying force) and all men from 16 to 70 who had not been born in the islands together with their families, were to be 'evacuated'. The following day the first 280 people embarked on a ship for St. Malo; 346 more followed on 18 September and the last group of approximately 500 left on 29 September. In Guernsey 825 men, women and children, including nine from Sark, left on the night of 25/26 and 28 September 1941.

The Germans appeared to be satisfied that Hitler's orders had been carried out. Then on the night of 3/4 October 1942, a small British Commando raid, code name Basalt, took place on Sark. Five Germans were captured and tied up. It was reported that in the struggle two were killed, two escaped and were shot at and the remaining prisoner was taken back to England along with the news of the deportations. A sixth soldier, a sentry also appeared to have been killed in the raid. Mrs. Pittard, a widow living in Sark, was imprisoned in Guernsey and later deported by the Germans for giving information to the raiders. With the discovery of the bound bodies, the German Supreme Command issued the following order: 'From noon on October 8th all British officers and men taken prisoner at Dieppe will be bound.' A total of 1,376 prisoners were shackled and the British in turn chained an equal number of German prisoners of war in Canada, until the Red Cross stepped in to put an end to tit for tat reprisals.

In February 1943, partly on the grounds of military security and using the Sark raid as an excuse, 200 more people were deported from the islands to cover up the punishment of Mrs. Pittard for her part in it. She was among the 47 people selected from Sark, mainly families living in the centre of the island where the Germans wanted to billet their troops for safety after the commando raid. Others selected included those with prison records, those with a military background, those who had offended the Germans, officials of societies and Jews. Deportation lists were compiled from records used for the issue of identification cards to which the Germans had access.

The ships left Jersey on 13 and 25 February 1943 with approximately 90 people aboard. The rest left Guernsey on the 12th and 25th. With them was Robert Hathaway, the American-born husband of the Dame of Sark and Ambrose Sherwill and his family. The former Attorney-General and President of the Controlling Committee had been relieved of his duties for his part in helping the British agents, Nicolles and Symes, and had served a short prison sentence.

The deportees went to internment camps in Germany, France and Austria (Source 20) the more important of which are listed below. These were set up with cookhouses, canteens, hospitals, storage block, concert and dance halls, sanitary facilities and, where appropriate, schoolrooms. The YMCA and Red Cross sent materials and equipment for recreational activities and even managed to send musical instruments.

DORSTEN: A transit camp was set up in a heavily bombed industrial area in the Ruhr. Conditions were extremely primitive and it was evacuated in November 1942. Denis Cleary, a deportee sent back to Jersey due to his state of health, gave a glowing account of camp life there. His interview was printed in the *Jersey Evening Post* on 13 November, and in the *Guernsey Star* on 19 November 1942, but from later accounts of life and conditions in the camps it was probably pure German propaganda.

In his book *The Silent War* Frank Falla wrote about the reaction of the two Guernsey reporters who interviewed him: 'Though Cleary denied the suggestion, it was patently obvious to both journalists that he had been 'got at' by the Germans and indoctrinated. Deportees writing back were emphatic that half of his story was sheer poppycock, and hinted that he had been brainwashed.'

BIBERACH: A prisoner of war camp for officers, situated on the River Riss in Southern Germany. (Source 24) Biberach was the largest of the internment camps and held about 1,000 people. The facilities were far better than Dorsten, but initially food was still a problem.

Before the Red Cross parcels arrived, each internee survived on a litre of hot liquid a day, watery vegetable soup, and bread. Inmates were housed in barracks (buildings) each of which had 84 internees crowded into it and, depending on the size of the room, between four and 18 prisoners in each. In comparison, the notorious camp of Auschwitz held 500 people in the same-size barrack.

The camp housed Guernsey and Jersey families with children up to the age of 16. A report from camp captain Garfield Garland to the Bailiff in Guernsey on conditions in Biberach was printed in the *Guernsey Evening Press*. (Source 21) He would have been obliged to make it sound encouraging to pass the German censors.

WURZACH: An 18th century castle, later a Catholic Monastery and then a priests' training college, south of Biberach. Jersey families numbering more than 600 men, women and children, were housed in overcrowded quarters. As in other camps rations consisted of a watery vegetable soup and a loaf of rye bread, shared between five people in the week and four on weekends. The internees were so hungry during the first few months that Michael Ginns, who was deported from Jersey at the age of 14 with his parents, remembers 'diving in the mud for the hard biscuits that the French prisoners of war were throwing over to us. You'd eat the biscuit, mud and all.' (Source 22)

It was not until December 1942 that the first Red Cross parcels arrived in the camps. These continued on a weekly basis until the end of 1944 and thereafter fortnightly. Apart from the loss of freedom, which was hard to bear, the internees were faring better than the civilian population in the Channel Islands. Michael Ginns's father, who suffered ill-health, probably survived the war only because he was deported. He was one of the elderly and sick internees who were repatriated to England in 1944.

His wife Emma Ginns a qualified nurse, was appointed matron of the Wurzach camp hospital. On their silver wedding anniversary she was presented by the internees with a scroll to mark the occasion and to acknowledge her hard work on their behalf. (Source 23)

Some of the internees eventually obtained permission to send Red Cross parcels back to the islands for their families. Mrs. Tremayne made reference to some of these arriving in Guernsey on 6 March 1943. When the International Red Cross discovered what the internees were doing they put a stop to it, pointing out the parcels were intended for internees and not for people in occupied countries.

Internees, however, managed to barter with some of the German guards, exchanging the surplus for fresh vegetables. Baskets containing tins of cocoa, soap or other items were lowered down the castle walls after dark. Also on weekly escorted walks outside the camps, some internees occasionally had the opportunity to barter with the local people and visit pubs.

As conditions got worse in the Channel Islands towards the latter part of 1943, Mrs. Tremayne wrote in her diary *War on Sark:* 'It is very strange because those people who were sent to Biberach and Laufen are having all sorts of luxuries to eat and to wear, and they all wish they could send something to us who were left behind.'

KREUZBURG: Formerly a criminal lunatic asylum situated near Breslau in Upper Silesia, not far from Auschwitz. Among the internees were approximately 80 Jews. But for the fact they carried British passports they would have been sent to the death camps.

LAUFEN: A centuries old castle on the River Salzac in Bavaria. (Source 25) Single men over the age of 16 were transferred there from other camps in October 1942. Sport was a particularly popular pastime. It was here that Major Ambrose Sherwill, former Attorney-General and President of the Controlling Committee, Guernsey, was interned. He later took over as camp leader from Frank Stroobant, a Guernseyman who had provided food on the quayside for the people during earlier deportations in September 1942. Roy Skingle, a Jerseyman, was deputy camp leader and it fell to him on one occasion to write and thank the Bailiff of Jersey on behalf of the camp for a very generous gift of 5,000 cigarettes. Grateful for the gift, he tactfully explained in the letter that their Red Cross supplies probably made them better off than their families and friends in Jersey and suggested the gift should not be repeated. (Source 26)

Liberation of all the internment camps began on 23 April 1945 (Source 27) but it was some months before the internees were repatriated to the Channel Islands.

Not to be forgotten are the political prisoners from the Channel Islands who suffered, (and some died) in penal prisons and concentration camps. Roger Harris devotes a chapter to these tragic people in his book *Islanders Deported.*

INTERNMENT CAMPS IN GERMANY

If entertainment was important in raising the morale of the people in the Channel Islands, it was even more so in the internment camps in Germany. These were enclosed camps in Germany where British-born people, deported from the Channel Islands by order of Hitler, were interned. The internees formed drama groups and orchestras (Source 28) and reports of theatrical and musical productions appeared in the Channel Islands' newspapers.

The Red Cross and the YMCA (Young Men's Christian Association) were allowed to send material and equipment for recreational activities in the camps. Nothing was wasted. The internees soon learned how to make stage sets for shows and plays out of empty

Red Cross cartons, packing cases and various other oddments.

Such was the spirit of the British prisoners in Biberach internment camp that they held carnivals inside the barbed wire compounds. They took part in fancy dress parades, using all their skills and ideas with the materials they were able to beg or borrow. Almost every barrack in the camp, consisting of the huts in which prisoners lived and slept, entered an exhibit in the parade and there were such characters as St. George and the Dragon, Cleopatra borne by blackened bearers, and South Sea Island natives wearing grass skirts.

Sport in Biberach was usually limited to rounders, cricket and handball as the ground was rocky and hard and made it dangerous to play football. (Source 29) In Laufen internment camp, where the ground conditions were better and many of the internees were young men, hockey, football and rugby were extremely popular and excess energy was worked off in friendly rivalry.

Lecturers, artists and tradesmen passed on their knowledge and skills to fellow internees, and the result was an extremely good standard of needlework, handwork, arts and crafts. Scrap metal and tins from Red Cross parcels were beaten into useful containers. (See Source 30)

In 1943 the internees in Laufen managed to construct a secret wireless receiver out of parts taken from an electrical store outside the camp. Using a 3-watt bulb and listening to the set under a blanket, a Guernseyman, Frank Stroobant, was able to listen to around 1,200 hours of BBC overseas news broadcasts. Rather appropriately the receiver was named 'The Forbidden Whisper'. (Source 31)

LIBERATION

Operation Nest Egg was the name under which Task Force 135 carried out the liberation of the Channel Islands. The War Office had first considered sending liberating forces in November 1943, but heavy anti-aircraft artillery on the islands made an air assault unlikely to succeed. An attack from the sea would have required a number of units urgently needed elsewhere at that time, and civilian casualties would have been heavy.

The Normandy landings on 6 June 1944 gave islanders every hope that liberation was close. But the Allies were kept busy pushing the German army further back towards Germany. It was to be almost another year before that freedom came.

Daily Life and Liberation

Supplies to the islands were cut off when the French ports fell to the allies. The British government's plan to starve the garrison out and force them to surrender became a long drawn out process. The RAF made repeated drops of propaganda leaflets over the islands urging German troops to surrender in the hope of demoralising them. By the end of 1944 siege conditions were approaching their worst. The population was cold and hungry and German troops suffered equally with vastly reduced rations. The once arrogant conquerors now looked like an army of ragamuffins.

The Red Cross ship SS *Vega* arrived just after Christmas 1944 with her first cargo of parcels. German troops had no right to any of these. Although they honoured the regulation, the military authorities cut the scant civilian rations even further, in effect benefiting from the mercy mission, a point which had concerned Winston Churchill when he first resisted the request for Red Cross supplies to be sent to the islands.

By the beginning of May 1945 the German army had been completely defeated. Brigadier Snow and his staff set sail for the Channel Islands aboard the British destroyer HMS *Bulldog* from Plymouth on 8 May in the company of HMS *Beagle*. The war was over, all but for the unconditional surrender of Vice-Admiral Hüffmeier in Guernsey and Major-Gemeral Wolfe in Jersey.

Hüffmeier made one last attempt for an armistice before he sent his Chief of Staff, Major-General Heine, to sign the surrender documents aboard HMS *Bulldog* at 7.15am on 9 May 1945. (Source 32) Brigadier Snow then sailed to Jersey aboard HMS *Beagle* where Major- General Wolfe signed a second document of surrender at 10am.

An initial landing party of two officers and twenty men went ashore on each of the two islands, to be followed by larger parties later in the day. They were greeted by jubilant islanders who turned out in their thousands to welcome them. (Source 33) Sark was liberated on 10 May but it was 16 May before troops from Task Force 135 landed on Alderney.

The main party of Task Force 135 arrived in the islands on 12 May (Source 34) and undertook the difficult job of returning them to normal civil control. German engineers under the supervision of the Royal Engineers were set to work to clear the vast number of land mines. According to situation reports in the Kew Public Record Office, as noted in the *Channel Islands Occupation Review 1985*, there were in all 177,925 mines laid in 305 minefields: Alderney 30,345, Guernsey

> Field Command
> St. Helier, 27th September, 1940.
>
> ORDER.
>
> A Purchasing Commission of the Central Foreign Department for furnishing Motor Vehicles to the Army in the occupied territories has arrived in Jersey to purchase motor vehicles owned on the Island. All motor vehicles, except those set aside for military purposes or the maintenance of the economic operations of the Island, are to be produced before this commission at a muster. A written receipt will be given for those vehicles which are found to be capable of being used and these motor vehicles are to be collected in a large garage ready to be loaded. Lists are to be prepared of the motor vehicles shown and it is to be stated in these lists whether the motor vehicles are in driving order or not. Motor vehicles which are out of order will be handed over for inspection by a technical inspector who will have them put into commission by the repair workshops of the Island.
>
> The motor vehicles are to be shown by the owner or authorised representative. The licence papers, as well as the certified accounts for purchases and repairs, from which the present value of the vehicle can be seen, are to be brought along.
>
> The Department of Transport and Communications of the States of Jersey is charged to make the arrangements necessary to give effect to this Order.
>
> For the Field Commander
> (Signed) JOHANNES, O.K.V.R.

Source 1: Extract of the military order for the compulsory purchase of motor vehicles. *Jersey Evening Post, dated 28.9.1940*

66,590, Jersey 67,883 and in Sark 13,107. A further 50,000 tons of ammunition also had to be disposed of.

The number of German troops in the islands had varied over the five years. The garrison, which was taken to the UK (Source 35) and mainly put to work on farms, amounted to 26,909: Guernsey 11,755, Jersey 11,611, Alderney 3,202 and Sark 281 *(Channel Islands Occupation Review 1985)*. About 3,000 of them were kept in the islands until the large scale mop-up operations had been completed.

The repatriation of islanders wishing to return to their homes was a lengthy process. People with skills were the first to return. (Source 36) Others had to wait until there was accommodation to house them. Many of the houses had been destroyed or were unfit to live in and it was Christmas 1945 before the people of Alderney were able to return to their homes. (Source 37)

The islands, however, were free at last. Records and memories and a legacy of concrete have been left to remind us of those long dark five years.

Source 2: The Emeralds in Guernsey. The timber structure of the radio station can be seen on top of the roof. *Photograph: Ozanne collection*

Source 3: A Jersey bus fitted with a French Brandt Gazogene charcoal producer gas system, October 1941.
Photograph: Jersey Evening Post

Source 4: German soldier riding a bicycle and trailer at Patriotic Street, Jersey.
Photograph: Société Jersiaise

Source 5: A specially constructed horse-drawn bus which operated in Jersey.
Photograph: Jersey Evening Post

Source 6: Horse-drawn van used by Lovell & Co Ltd in Guernsey to move furniture.
Photograph: Carel Toms Collection

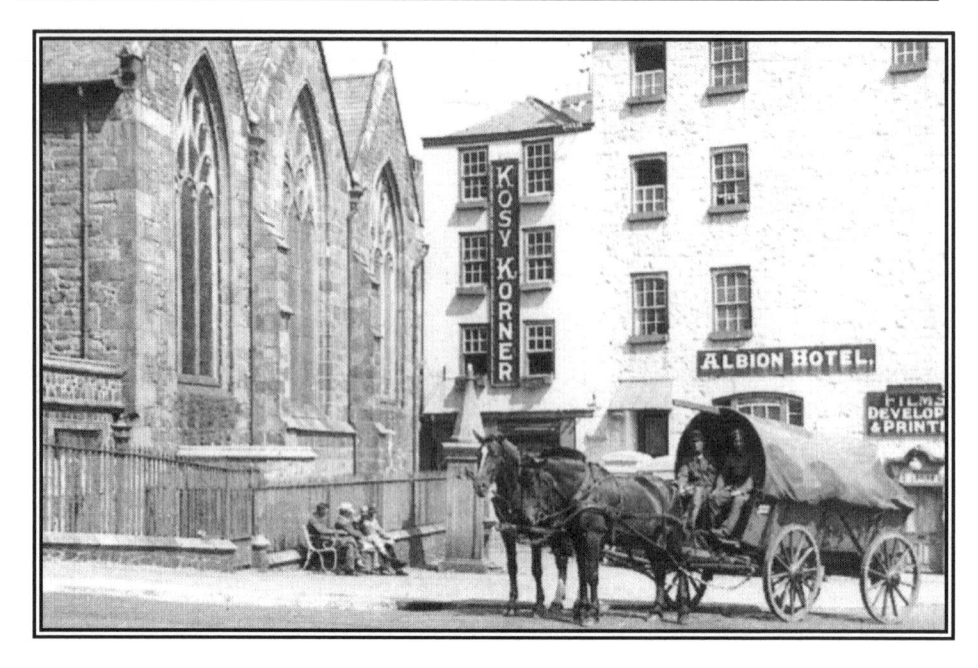

Aspects of War

Source 7: German soldiers driving a horse-drawn cart in St. Peter Port, Guernsey.
Photograph: Carel Toms Collection

Source 8: Organisation Todt workers laying railway lines near the abbatoirs in Jersey.
Photograph: CIOS Jersey Collection

Source 9: German officers of Field Command 515 riding some of the fine German horses imported into the islands during the Occupation, overlooking Gorey Harbour, Jersey. *Photograph: Carel Toms Collection*

```
Households of:-
1 person without gas or electricity for cooking    1 cwt. wood
2 to 6                                             2 cwt. wood
7 or more                                          3 cwt. wood
1 person with gas or electricity for cooking       NIL
2 to 4                                             NIL
5 or more                                          NIL
Persons age 75 or over, medical reasons            NIL **
Babies under 18 months of age                      1 cwt. wood
   ** covered by an emergency ration of other fuel.
```

Source 10: State of Guernsey Report on the essential supplys and services during the Occupation.

Aspects of War

Source 11: (Above) Cutting peat at Vazon, Guernsey.
Photograph: Carel Toms Collection

(Below) Peat cut and stacked at L'Etacq, Jersey.
Photograph: Société Jersiaise

Source 12: Mr. Henry Grube of the Jersey Evening Post with Sonderfuhrer Hohl, the German censor.
Photograph: Bundesarchiv

SHORTAGE OF NEWSPRINT

Owing to the acute shortage of newsprint, it has been mutually agreed between the two local newspapers that but one paper will be published each day, as follows:

The "Guernsey Evening Press"
on Mondays, Wednesdays and Fridays

The "Guernsey Star"
on Tuesdays, Thursdays and Saturdays

This decision has the approval of the German Authorities and the States Controlling Committee, and will take effect as from Monday next, the 26th instant.

In order to maintain the present Staffs and Newsvendors the price of the papers will be increased to 2d.

It is particularly emphasised that a direct order should be given to your usual newsagent, as it is impossible to supply these with any unordered copies.

Copies of all the Official announcements will be displayed daily in the windows of both Newspapers.

Source 13: This notice appeared in the Guernsey Evening Press dated 24.2.1942 informing its readers that with the approval of the German authorities, future issues would appear three times a week on alternate days to the Star.

Source 14: Earpieces were taken from telephone boxes to be used with crystal sets.

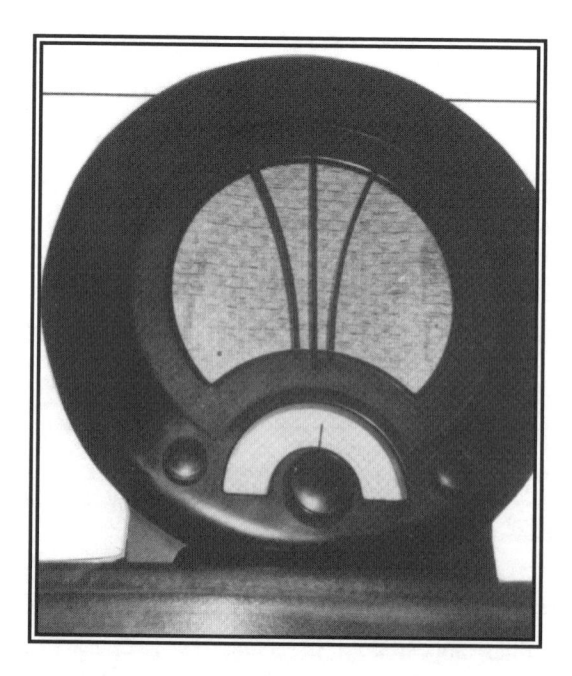

Source 15: Example of a radio set used during the Occupation.
German Occupation Museum

Vol. X. No. 33.   Friday, September 3rd, 1943.   9 p.m.

ITALY.--Allied troops were still crossing the Straits of Messina for the invasion of the Italian mainland at 10 o'clock this morning, the first troops having landed at 4.30 this morning under cover of a terrific bombardment by land, sea and air. The troops landed are those of the British and Canadian 8th Army. No official news of our troops progress has yet come to hand and it is not known where, on the Italian mainland, the landings were made. The Axis say they were made at San Giovanni and Reggio. Yesterday General Eisenhower, who is in charge of operations, flew to Sicily for last-minute consultations with Generals Alexander and Montgomery. Correspondents report that our troops are in for some stiff fighting with mountainous country (favourable for demolition work aiding the enemy. We have definite sea and air superiority. Adter two weeks rest our troops are confident and in fine fettle. No mention has been made of American troops. Our bombers and fighters have kept up their recent pounding of the enemy's rail communications and have attacked his troops and gun emplacements. In the North of Italy, too, we have made very heavy attacks on communications. Biggest attacks were made by American Flying Fortresses which have attacked and seriously damaged at several points the main railway from Germany to Italy at the Brenner Pass. Most of the Nazi traffic comes over here and after the Americans' attack the lines were littered with wreckage. At Trento the railway was cut by four direct hits while heaviest damage by the Fortresses was at Bolognia. Here strong fighter opposition was encountered and we shot down 23 of the enemy for the loss of ten. From all operations we lost 15 aircraft and destroyed 35 of the enemy. In his message to the 8th Army before they attacked the Commander said:--"We have a good plan and air support. We have only one end in view. We mean to knock Italy right out of the war."

FRANCE.--Home-based bombers and fighters have made morning and afternoon raids on varied targets in Northern France. Fortresses raided a place outside Paris. Thunderbolts attacked airfields escorted by Spitfires. While the latter made sweeps over targets. Heavy opposition was encountered.

ALLIED aircaft dropped 200 tons of bombs on a Japanese headquarters at Madani. During the period July--August we destroyed 584 Japanese planes for the loss of 145.

CHURCHES of all religions in England observe today as a special day of prayer.

MR. CHURCHILL and President Roosevelt have continued their conference at Washington.

RUSSIA.--The Soviet communique reports more progress on 5 fronts particularly in the Donetz Basin. 150 places have been captured in advances of 10 to 12 miles. In the wedge they have established between the German Northern and Southern Armies the Russians have advanced 12 miles and have taken places ahead of Sumy. Kenetep 40 miles West of Sumy has also been taken. The Russian cut of the Briansk-Kiev railway has been extended. On the Briansk front 60 villages have been taken in advances of from 4 to 6 miles against strong enemy opposition.

DENMARK.-The German-controlled Danish Radio reports further acts of sabotage in the capital, Copenhagen. This morning curfew has been extended and now is 9 at night until 6 in the morning. 150 cases of curfew infractions occurred in Copenhagen last night. The death penalty is threatened to all those who retain firearms.

SATURDAY, SEPTEMBER 4th, 7 a.m.

BERLIN.- Our bombers attacked targets in Berlin last night.

RUSSIA.- The Germans are in full retreat in the Donetz though they have counter-attacked in other sectors.

ITALY.- There is no official news from Italy this morning.

Source 16: Copy of a Guernsey Underground News Sheet

RED CROSS MESSAGES

INTERESTING FIGURES FOR FIRST YEAR'S WORKING

Between January 13th, 1940, and the tenth day of the present month the local Red Cross Department had handled no fewer than 53,683 incoming messages from overseas friends and relatives or islanders. The same number of replies has been sent, making a total of 107,366 messages dealt with in this way within the twelve-month.

In addition to this colossal correspondence, since the inauguration of the Monthly Family Message Scheme on July 14th, of last year, 46,084 messages have been dispatched, despite several breaks of varying intervals.

These records show how greatly appreciated has been the service of the International Red Cross in this respect and the thanks of the public are due to Mr. G. A. Bradshaw, who has organised the working of the local branch, as well as to his staff of paid assistants and that other willing band of volunteer helpers who are always on duty in rotation throughout the week.

Mrs. Louise Le Page, "Elmside," Castel, from her daughter, Mrs. Wilma Bougourd: "Glad to hear from you but wanting more; both Simpson Fielden families well." Huddersfield September 3.

Mrs. A. Huddle, 1, "Victoria Place," Victoria Road, from her daughter, Betty: "Having a lovely time; very well cared for," with enquiry and greetings. October 7.

Mrs. Mahy, "Parkstone," Pontinfer, from Mrs. Robinson: Enquiry and "We are all right; your flowers are out; it reminds us of our happy times." October 9.

Mr. Le Tissier, "Les Goddards," Vazon, from his daughter, Rosemary "Am well with Mummy, Auntie Annie," with greetings also to relatives. August 22.

Mr. and Mrs. P. Le Cras, Sous l'Eglise, St. Saviour's, from their daughter, Amy, in Canada: Enquiry and "Writing to Julia's daughters," with greetings also from "Jim and family." September 22.

Mr. and Mrs. S. Marquand, 7 Union Street, first message from their children, Barbara and Roy (Br— Lane School): "Well, happy of Stanley (their eldest son Joseph's School); er growin' eat, sl——
enqu—
Sen—

Source 17: Red Cross messages from relatives and friends printed in the Guernsey Evening Press dated 17.1.1942

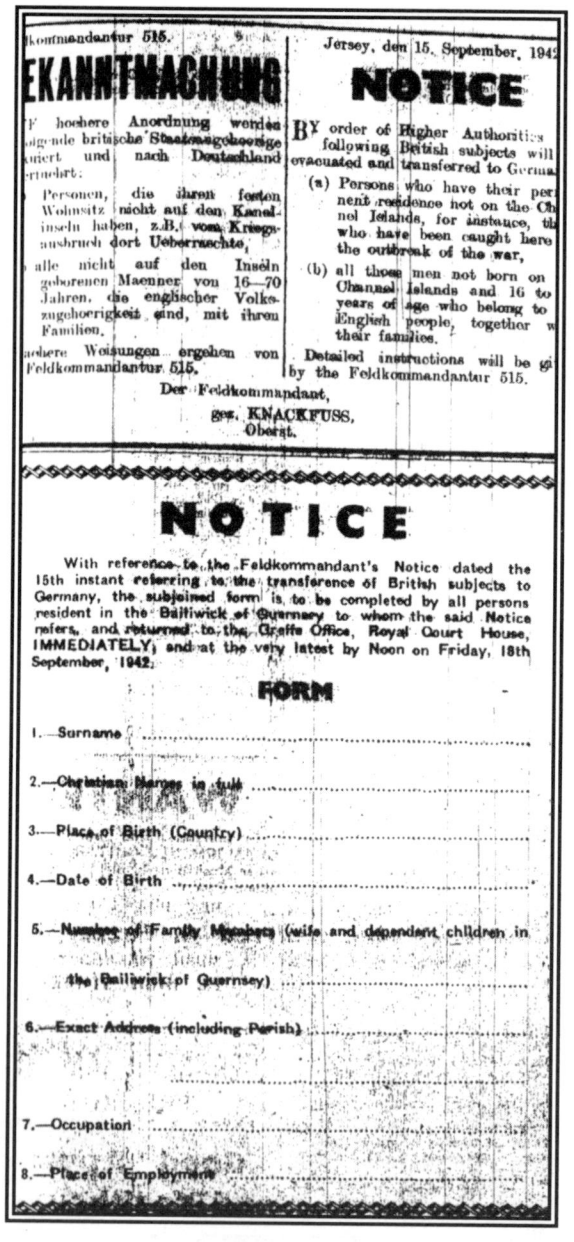

Kommandantur 515.

BEKANNTMACHUNG

Jersey, den 15. September, 1942

F— hochere Anordnung werden —igende britische Staatsangehoerige —uiert und nach Deutschland —fuehrt:

Personen, die ihren festen Wohnsitz nicht auf den Kanalinseln haben, z.B. vom Kriegsausbruch dort Ueberraschte,

alle nicht auf den Inseln geborenen Maenner von 16—70 Jahren, die englischer Volkszugehoerigkeit sind, mit ihren Familien.

—adere Weisungen ergehen von Feldkommandantur 515.

Der Feldkommandant,
ggz. KNACKFUSS,
Oberst.

NOTICE

BY order of Higher Authorities following British subjects will evacuated and transferred to Germa—

(a) Persons who have their permanent residence not on the Channel Islands, for instance, th— who have been caught here the outbreak of the war,

(b) all those men not born on Channel Islands and 16 to years of age who belong to English people, together w— their families.

Detailed instructions will be gi— by the Feldkommandantur 515.

NOTICE

With reference to the Feldkommandant's Notice dated the 15th instant referring to the transference of British subjects to Germany, the subjoined form is to be completed by all persons resident in the Bailiwick of Guernsey to whom the said Notice refers, and returned to the Greffe Office, Royal Court House, IMMEDIATELY, and at the very latest by Noon on Friday, 18th September, 1942.

FORM

1. — Surname ....
2. — Christian Names in full ....
3. — Place of Birth (Country) ....
4. — Date of Birth ....
5. — Number of Family Members (wife and dependant children in the Bailiwick of Guernsey) ....
6. — Exact Address (including Parish) ....
7. — Occupation ....
8. — Place of Employment ....

Source 18: The 'evacuation' notice (the word deportation was not used), appeared in the Jersey Evening Post on 15.9.1942. The same notice appeared in the Guernsey Evening Press on the following day but with the addition of a form.

Daily Life and Liberation

A photograph of Rosemary and David Hamon, taken while they were evacuated to Lancashire.

Source 19: Red Cross message sent to two children, Rosemary and David Hamon, evacuated to Lancashire with their mother in 1940. The two names in the signature were combined to keep the message to 25 words.

Source 20: Typical living quarters in an internment camp.
German Occupation Museum

Married Camp in Germany has Ample Money, Food and Clothing

The true state of affairs in the Camp at B——, Germany, is admirably explained by Mr. Garfield Garland, Camp Senior, in a letter to the Bailiff.

(Letter to the Editor)

Sir,—I enclose copy of a letter which I have received to-day from Mr. G. G. Garland, Camp Commandant at B——, and which I would be grateful if you would publish in your next issue. I do not propose to send any further contributions of my Second Fund to this Camp until a further appeal for money is made by Mr. Garland. The Camp at L—— appears to be in somewhat an analagous position, but Mr. Stroobant, the Camp Commandant there, appeals for money for the purchase of medical and dental supplies which the poorer internees of the Camp are unable to afford to procure for themselves. I am therefore applying a portion of the fund for this purpose, besides keeping in touch with the other internment camps where our fellow Islanders have gone.

VICTOR G. CAREY,
Bailiff.

The Bailiff's Chambers,
Guernsey.
March 26, 1943.

MR. GARFIELD GARLAND'S LETTER

In his letter Mr. Garland writes extremely reassuringly as follows: —

Dear Mr. Bailiff,—I thank you for your letter of the 8th of February received on the 20th instant. On behalf of the Camp I thank you and those kind friends who have subscribed to the fund being put at our disposal for those of us who are in need.

I would point out that we have been presented by various British officers, who are prisoners of war, with the sum of **RMS. 5,500**, which is being held as a reserve for incidental camp expenses for the time being. We have also been allowed by the Swiss Government the sum of 10 RMS. per head per month, which enables us to make purchases from the canteen.

We are now in a better financial position than we were when first funds were mooted. Our present requirements are therefore well catered for and I feel it would be an imposition to call upon the already over-taxed generosity of our friends for further contributions at the moment.

Circumstances of course might not always be the same and in such an eventuality we might be glad to call for your kind assistance. We have also been provided with a considerable amount of clothing, which should satisfy our needs at the moment.

With regard to food I feel we are better provided for than are most of our friends in Guernsey and it would be a definite imposition to accept any assistance from the island in this respect at present.

Kindly accept the best wishes and greetings of all Guernsey Internees and convey them also to our many friends still with you.

(Signed) G. G. GARLAND,
Camp Captain.

23rd February, 1943.

Source 21: Extract from Guernsey Evening Press, dated 29.3.1943

Source 22: Internee identification card issued to Michael Ginns in Biberach before he was moved to Wurzach.
Courtesy: Michael Ginns, Jersey

Source 23: The scroll presented to Emma Ginns by the grateful internees of Wurzach August 1944.
Courtesy: Michael Ginns, Jersey

Source 24: Barracks at Biberach where the deportees were housed.
Photograph: CIOS Guernsey Collection

Source 25: The castle at Laufen where men over the age of 16 were interned.
Photograph: CIOS Guernsey Collection

Daily Life and Liberation

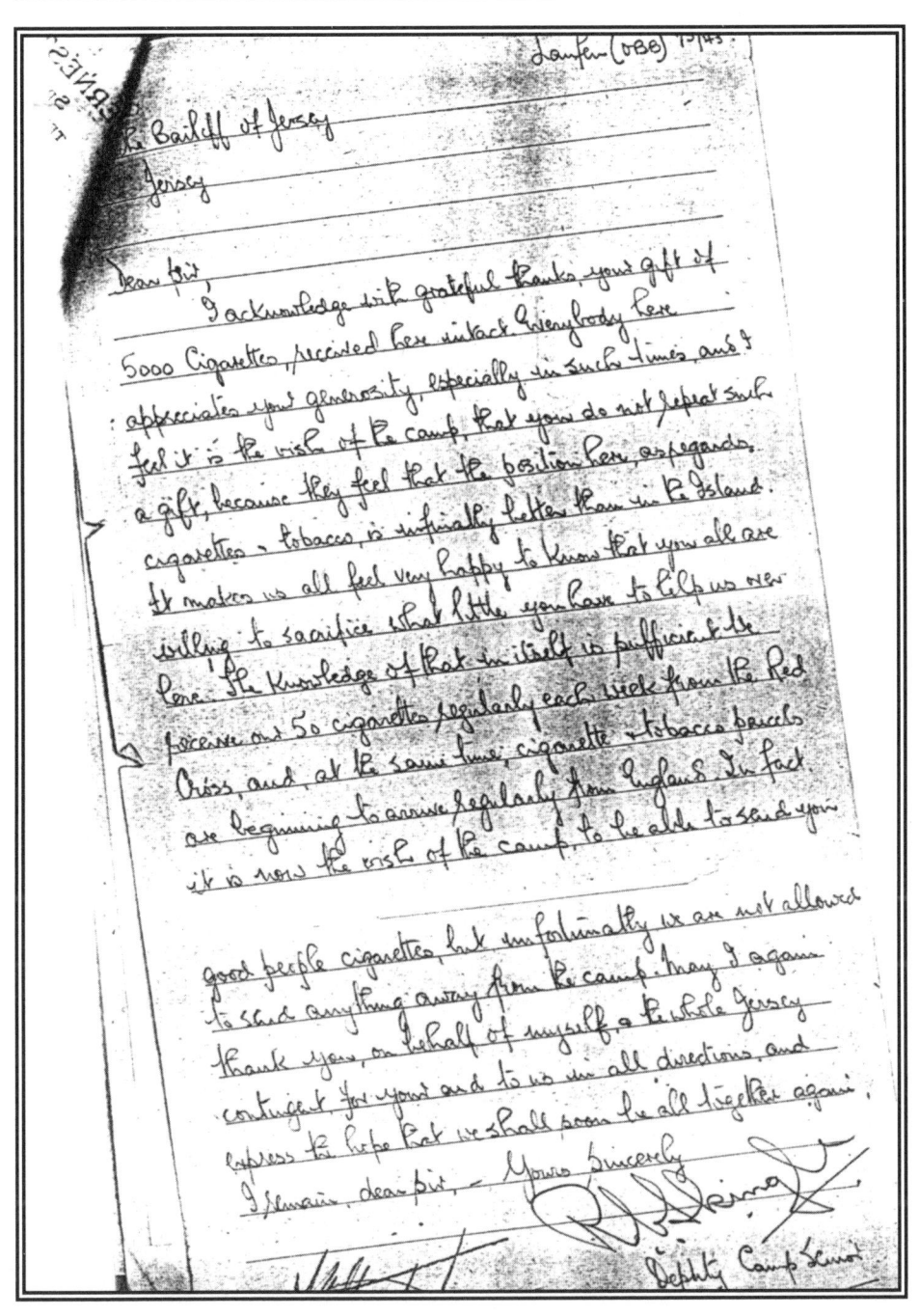

> Laufen (OBS) 13/43
>
> R. Bailiff of Jersey
> Jersey
>
> Dear Sir,
>
> I acknowledge with grateful thanks your gift of 5000 Cigarettes, received here intact. Everybody here appreciates your generosity, especially in such times, and I feel it is the wish of the camp, that you do not repeat such a gift, because they feel that the position here as regards cigarettes + tobacco, is infinitely better than in the Island. It makes us all feel very happy to know that you all are willing to sacrifice what little you have to help us over here. The knowledge of that in itself is sufficient to foresee. We get 50 cigarettes regularly each week from the Red Cross, and at the same time, cigarette + tobacco parcels are beginning to arrive regularly from England. In fact it is now the wish of the camp, to be able to send you good people cigarettes, but unfortunately we are not allowed to send anything away from the camp. May I again thank you, on behalf of myself + the whole Jersey contingent for your aid to us in all directions, and express the hope that we shall soon be all together again.
>
> I remain, dear sir, — Yours sincerely
>
> [signature]
> Deputy Camp Senior

Source 26: Letter to the Bailiff of Jersey from Jerseyman Roy Skingle deputy camp leader to Guernseyman Frank Stroobant in Laufen. The position was later taken over by Major Sherwill, later to become Sir Ambrose Sherwill.
Document: Jersey Archives Service

Aspects of War

Source 27: Liberation of Laufen.
Photograph: CIOS Guernsey Collection

Source 28: The Camp Orchestra in Biberach Internment Camp, Germany
Photograph: Mrs. D. R. Mees, Guernsey

Daily Life and Liberation

Source 29: Football team at Biberach Internment Camp, Germany 1943-44
Photograph: CIOS Collection, Guernsey

Source 30: Child's stove, pots and pans made from scrap metal and empty Red Cross tins for Rose Daw by her father whilst they were interned at Biberach.
Photograph: The German Occupation Museum

Source 31: 'The Forbidden Whisper' Taken after the liberation of Laufen Camp with Guernseyman Frank Stroobant, left, and Jerseyman Billy Williams, right. Another Jerseyman, Bill Drinkwater was invited to help in the making of the set.
Photograph: German Occupation Museum

Source 32: The terms of surrender are read to Major General Heine, Chief of Staff to Vice-Admiral Hüffmeier, on board HMS Bulldog anchored off St. Peter Port, Guernsey.
Photograph: Imperial War Museum

Daily Life and Liberation

Source 33: Islanders welcoming the liberating forces in Guernsey. Photograph: Carel Toms Collection

Source 34: Islanders flocked to West Park, St. Helier, to greet the arrival of Task Force 135 on 12 May 1945. Much of the transport was horse-drawn, all still driving on the righthand side of the road, as ordered by the German authorities. *Photograph: Carel Toms Collection*

Aspects of War

Source 35: German prisoners of war in Jersey embarking on landing ships which brought the liberation forces to the Channel Islands.
Photograph: Société Jersiaise

Source 36: Alderney at the time of liberation.
Photograph: Carel Toms Collection

NOTICE

Relative to the Return of Skilled Evacuees.

In view of the colossal amount of work required on building in this Island before the majority of our evacuees can return to Guernsey, the Ministry of Labour will expedite the return of "key" men (i.e. skilled workers in the building and allied trades — carpenters, joiners, plumbers, plasterers, slaters, masons, painters, etc.) In order to obtain the necessary permission for these to return to the Island, all employers of labour in the building and allied trades and also in the professions must notify the Labour Officer, Hirzel House, of any key employee for whom they desire an early return.

The following information should be given:—

1. Name and present address of employee.
2. A statement that he or she is a key employee, giving particulars of trade.
3. That the employee has expressed a desire to return.

This information is being collected on behalf of the Immigration and Emigration Officer, Ladies' College, to whom all other enquiries must be addressed.

R. H. JOHNS,
Labour Officer.

Hirzel House,
Guernsey.
2nd June, 1945. (943

Source 37: Guernsey Evening Press dated 2.6.1945

	REGISTRATION FORM.		Denoting Letter and Number of Place of Issue to be entered here
	Two copies of this Form must be completed by every person. If you are in doubt as to how to complete this Form, the Constable or a Douzenier of your Parish will help you.	For Official use only. No. 20587	

(a) Surname in block letters followed by Christian names. — (a) HELYER VICTOR GEORGE
(b) Ordinary Postal address, including Parish — (b) THE NOOK, LA DOUVEE, JERBOURG, ST MARTIN
(c) Date of Birth — (c) 5/11/1909
(d) Place of Birth — (d) GUERNSEY
(e) Nationality* — (e) BRITISH
(f) Occupation — (f) BAKER & CONFECTIONER
(g) Single, married, widow or widower — (g) MARRIED
(h) Colour of hair — (h) LIGHT BROWN
(i) Colour of eyes — (i) BLUE

(j) Any physical peculiarities, such as a scar, limp, etc. — (j) NO
(k) Have you served in any of His Britannic Majesty's Armed Forces? If so, write R.N., R.N.R., Army, R.A.F., Royal Guernsey Militia, or as is appropriate and give your rank on retirement and the date of retirement. — (k) NO
(l) Are you on a Reserve of Officers of His Britannic Majesty's Armed Forces? If so, state which Reserve — (l) NO
(m) Are you, not being on a Reserve of Officers, on the Reserve of any of His Britannic Majesty's Armed Forces? If so, state which Reserve. — (m) NO

*As regards question (e), if you are a person possessing dual nationality, give both nationalities.

	RELATIONSHIP	NAME	RANK	BRANCH OF SERVICE
(n) Have you a husband, son, grandson, brother, father, nephew, uncle, or first cousin actually serving in any of His Britannic Majesty's Armed Forces? If so, give his relationship to you and his full name and rank and state which branch (such as R.N., Army, R.A.F., or as the case may require) of the Forces he belongs to. Do not give his Unit or any particulars of his last known whereabouts.		No		

If this space for your answer is insufficient, complete your answer on the reverse

	RELATIONSHIP	NAME
(o) Have you a husband, son, grandson, brother, father, nephew, uncle or first cousin who is, to your knowledge, on a Reserve of Officers of His Britannic Majesty's Armed Forces? If so, give his relationship to you and his full name and address.		No

(p) Having completed the answers to the *above* questions (and where the answer to any of word "No" must be written) take this Form to a Constable or Douzenier of your Parish take it to the Seneschal) and write your usual signature in his presence and add the date

(Signature) V.G. Helyer   Helyer
(Date) Oct 28/10/1940

Your signature must be witnessed by the Official before whom it is signed and he will sign his name and add his official title and the name of the Parish of which he is an Official.

Witnessed by A. Luing
(Signature)
Douzenier (Title)
St Martins (Name of Parish)

Identity Card issued by _____ (Official issuing Identity Card to insert his initials.)
Star Typ., Bordage—60m/10/1940.

Source 38: Example of a Guernsey registration form used for the issue of identity cards to Islands from October 1940 onwards, as directed by the German Military Authorities. Dependent children under the age of 14 did not have a card but details were declared on the reverse of the parents' forms. In 1942 a special form came into use for recording these details. Registration forms, to which the Germans had access, were used to compile deportation lists.

Courtesy: Island Archives Service

APPENDIX:

Example of a Guernsey registration form used for the issue of identity cards to Islanders from October 1940 onwards, as directed by the German military authorities. Dependent children under the age of 14 did not have a card but details were declared on the reverse of the parents' forms. In 1941 a special form came into use for recording these details. Registration forms, to which the Germans had access, were used to compile deportation lists. Courtesy: Island Archives Services

Select Bibliography

Bihet, Molly, *A Child's War* - (Guernsey Press 1985)
Banks, A.L. and Magee, H.E. (Effects of Enemy Occupation on the State of Health and Nutrition in the Channel Isles - (Bulletin of the Ministry of Health, September 1945)
Chalker, Bryan, *Out of the Frying Pan into Der Führer* - (Redcliffe Press, 1989)
Channel Islands Occupation Reviews:
    1979 - Sark Raid - Michael Ginns
    1984 - Bradshaw Advice Cards (and Red Cross Message Bureau) Guernsey, A.G. Marriner (CISS)
    1985 - Liberation - Leslie Jackson, John Wallbridge, Michael Ginns
    1986 - Sark Raid - Photographic postscript - Michael Ginns
    1988 - Evacuation of Guernsey Schoolchildren - Paul Le Pelley
Cortvriend, V.V., *Isolated Island: A History and Personal Reminiscences of the German Occupation of the Island of Guernsey, June 1940 - May 1945* - (Guernsey Star and Gazette, 1946)
Cruickshank, Charles, *The German Occupation of the Channel Islands* - (Oxford University Press for Imperial War Museum, 1979)
Durand, Ralph, *Guernsey under German Rule* - (The Guernsey Society, London 1946)
Falla, Frank, *The Silent War* - (Leslie Frewin,1967; Burbridge Limited, 1981)
Franks, Xan (ed.), *War on Sark: The Secret Letters of Julia Tremayne* - (Webb & Bower, 1981)
Ginns, Michael, *The Organisation Todt and the Fortress Engineers in the Channel Islands,* Archive Book No. 8 (CIOS Jersey Branch 1994)
Harris, Roger E., *Islanders Deported, Part 1* - (Channel Islands Specialists Society, 1980)

Mahy, Miriam, *There is an Occupation* - (Guernsey Press 1992)
Marshall, M., *Hitler Invaded Sark* - (Paramount-Lithoprint)
Maughan, R.C.F. *Jersey Under the Jackboot* - (New English Library, 1968)
Mayne, Richard, *Channel Islands Occupied* - (Jarrold 1981)
McKenzie, Donald, *Red Cross Mail Service for C.I. Civilians 1940-1945* - (Picton Publishing 1975)
Mollet, Ralph, *Jersey Under the Swastika* - (Hyperion Press, 1945)
Ramsey, Winston G., *The War in the Channel Islands Then and Now* (After the Battle, 1981: Battle of Britain Prints International Limited)
Sinel, Leslie P., *The German Occupation of Jersey. A complete Diary of Events June 1940-June 1945* (Jersey Evening Post, 1945)
Société Jersiaise, *The German Occupation of Jersey, 1940-1945*
States of Guernsey, Report on Essential Supplies and Services during the Occupation of Guernsey, - (Guernsey Star and Gazette, 1945)
States of Jersey Education Department, Occupation Resources 1985
Stroobant, Frank, *One Man's War* - (Guernsey Press 1967)
Toms, Carel, *Hitler's Fortress Islands* - (New English Library 1967)
Tough, Ken, *The States of Guernsey 1939-1945* (CIOS, Guernsey Branch)
Tremayne, Julia, see Franks, Xan
Trouteaud, Léonie D., Memories of Léonie D. Troutead, MBE, British Red Cross Society, Bailiwick of Guernsey Branch, (1993)
Wilson, Frank E., *Railways in Guernsey* - (Private Publication, Guernsey)
Wood, Alan and Mary, *Islands in Danger* - (Evans Brothers 1955)
The B. C. de Guerin Scrapbook (held at the Priaulx Library, Guernsey)
Guernsey Evening Press, newspapers covering 1940 - 1945
Guernsey Star and Gazette newspapers covering 1940- 1945
Jersey Evening Post, newspapers covering 1940 - 1945
Ord. Reverend, Unpublished diaries covering the German Occupation of Guernsey (held at the Priaulx Library, Guernsey)

About the Author

June Money was born in Guernsey in 1937 and remained on the Island with her parents during the five years of German Occupation.

After liberation in 1945 she moved with her family to London. On leaving school she eventually worked for a fashion magazine before moving on to a London newspaper and then an advertising agency.

She spent five years in Canada before returning to London and then Guernsey in the late 1960's with her husband and three children. She was divorced and subsequently married her late husband, Francis Money.

June has written a number of short stories for children which have been published in magazines, televised on national television and broadcast on local radio.

Some other Occupation titles from Channel Island Publishing

Living With The Enemy
Published in 1995, this book about the German Occupation of the Channel Islands has hit the No.1 spot every year as the best-selling local book.

Price inc. P&P to the UK £8.25

A Doctor's Occupation
First published in 1982 by Transworld Publishers, this well known Occupation book, published locally from 1997, is still a firm favourite.

Price inc. P&P to the UK £6.50

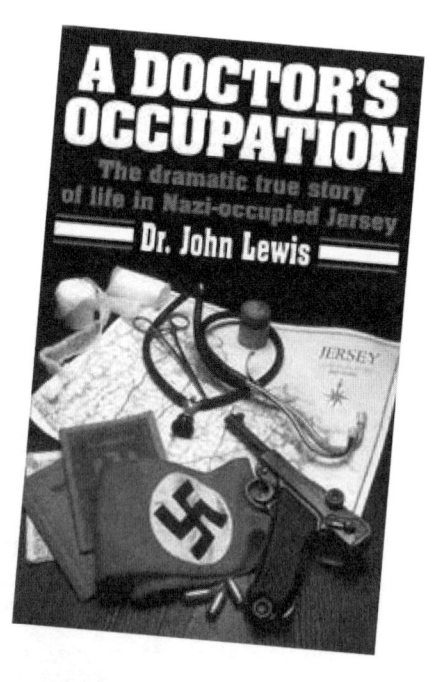

Channel Island Publishing
UNIT 3B, BARETTE COMMERCIAL CENTRE
LA ROUTE DU MONT MADO
ST.JOHN, JERSEY, CHANNEL ISLANDS, JE3 4DS

TEL 44 (0)1534 860806 FAX 44 (0)1534 860811
E-MAIL chris@channelislandpublishing.com

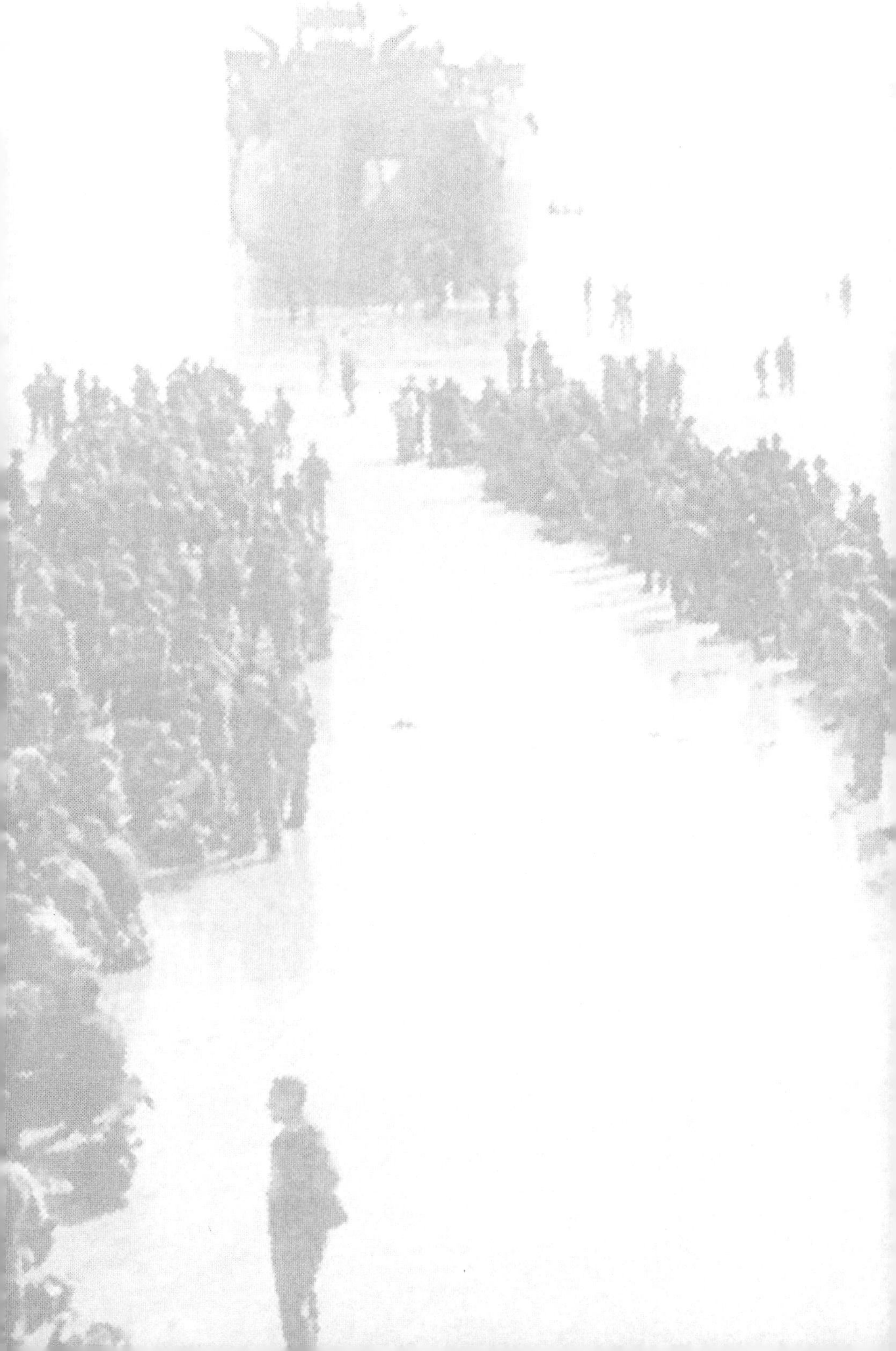